Getting Started in Computing for the Older Generation — Windows 7 Edition

Jim Gatenby

BERNARD BABANI (publishing) LTD
The Grampians
Shepherds Bush Road
London W6 7NF
England

www.babanibooks.com

D0620438

Please Note

Although every care has been taken with the production of this book to ensure that any projects, designs, modifications and/or programs, etc., contained herewith, operate in a correct and safe manner and also that any components specified are normally available in Great Britain, the Publishers and Author do not accept responsibility in any way for the failure (including fault in design) of any project, design, modification or program to work correctly or to cause damage to any equipment that it may be connected to or used in conjunction with, or in respect of any other damage or injury that may be so caused, nor do the Publishers accept responsibility in any way for the failure to obtain specified components.

Notice is also given that if equipment that is still under warranty is modified in any way or used or connected with home-built equipment then that warranty may be void.

© 2010 BERNARD BABANI (publishing) LTD

First Published – August 2010

Reprinted – December 2010

British Library Cataloguing in Publication Data:

A catalogue record for this book

ISBN 978-0-85934-717-4

Cover Design by Gregor Ar[...]

Printed and bound in Great [...]

Preface

The benefits of using your own computer can be enormous at any age, but especially so later in life. However, if you've little or no experience in this field, the idea of buying and starting to use a computer can be very daunting. This book aims to help the inexperienced user to choose a suitable computing setup for their own home so they can begin to enjoy the many new opportunities this will bring. For example, communicating with friends and family anywhere in the world using e-mail, finding the latest information on any subject and getting bargain prices from the Internet, editing and printing your own photographs or starting your own business working from home.

Computing is laden with jargon such as "gigabytes" and "dual-core processors", for example, and many of us find this off-putting. Some jargon is unavoidable and this is explained throughout the text. Chapter 9, "The Anatomy of a Computer", provides a deeper explanation of some of the more technical topics. The main components common to all computers and the associated jargon are explained; Chapter 9 is intended to be referred to when unfamiliar terms are encountered in the text.

Early chapters discuss connecting and setting up one or more computers and how to get online to the Internet using a device called a *wireless router*. The Windows 7 operating system controls everything done by the computer and this is discussed in detail, together with Windows' help for users with special needs, etc. The installation and use of essential software such as Microsoft Office is also covered. A later chapter gives advice for maintaining your computer and preventing attack from hackers and viruses. Although this book was prepared using Windows 7, much of the material is equally relevant to other versions of the Microsoft Windows operating system.

This book is by the same author as the best-selling and highly acclaimed "Computing for the Older Generation" (BP601).

About the Author

Jim Gatenby trained as a Chartered Mechanical Engineer and initially worked at Rolls-Royce Ltd using computers in the analysis of jet engine performance. He obtained a Master of Philosophy degree in Mathematical Education by research at Loughborough University of Technology and taught mathematics and computing in school for many years before becoming a full-time author. His most recent teaching posts included Head of Computer Studies and Information Technology Coordinator. The author has written many books in the fields of educational computing and Microsoft Windows, including many of the titles in the highly successful Older Generation series from Bernard Babani (publishing) Ltd.

The author has considerable experience of teaching students of all ages and abilities, in school and in adult education. For several years he successfully taught the well-established CLAIT course and also GCSE Computing and Information Technology.

Trademarks

Microsoft, Windows, Windows XP, Windows Vista, Windows 7, Windows Live Mail, Office 2010, Word and Excel are either trademarks or registered trademarks of Microsoft Corporation. Norton AntiVirus and Norton 360 are trademarks of Symantec Corporation. F-Secure Internet Security is a trademark or registered trademark of F-Secure Corporation. Kaspersky Internet Security is a trademark of Kaspersky Lab. BT is a registered trademark of British Telecommunications plc.

All other brand and product names used in this book are recognized as trademarks or registered trademarks, of their respective companies.

Acknowledgements

I would like to thank my wife Jill and our son David for their help and support during the preparation of this book.

Contents

5

6

Conventions Used in this Book

Words which appear on the screen in menus, etc., are shown in the text in bold, for example, **Print Preview**.

Certain words appear on the screen using the American spelling, such as **Disk Cleanup** for example. Where the text refers directly to an item displayed on the screen, the American spelling is used.

Mouse Operation

Throughout this book, the following terms are used to describe the operation of the mouse:

Click

A single press of the left-hand mouse button.

Double-click

Two presses of the left-hand mouse button, in rapid succession.

Right-click

A single press of the right-hand mouse button. Right-clicking an object on the screen, such as a picture, normally displays a "context-sensitive" pop-up menu with options relevant to the selected object.

Drag and Drop

Keep the left-hand or right-hand button held down and move the mouse, before releasing the button to transfer a screen object to a new position.

Further Reading

If you enjoy reading this book and find it helpful, you may be interested in the companion book by the same author, **An Introduction to the Internet for the Older Generation (BP711)** from Bernard Babani (publishing) Ltd and available from all good bookshops.

Computers in the Home

Introduction

Whatever your previous experience, there's never been a better time to get involved in computing, for the following reasons:

- Computers are nowadays much easier to use — you no longer need to be a "geek" or technical expert.
- Computing equipment is cheaper than ever before.
- There is an abundance of good software for every conceivable task.
- The Internet has created a wealth of opportunities for learning, leisure and working from home.

This chapter looks at some of the ways you might use computers in the home and in particular:

- Choosing between a laptop or desktop computer.
- Deciding on suitable location(s) in your home.
- Connecting the cables and starting up.

Not long ago, laptops were inferior to desktop computers in several respects. Recently, however, laptops have improved and are currently outselling desktop machines. If you want to use a computer on the move, in hotels and on the train, for example, then the laptop is the only choice. If your computer will mostly remain in one place in your home or office, then the desktop machine may be a better option.

Computing jargon has been avoided wherever possible in this book; explanations of essential jargon are given at the end of some chapters, where necessary. For more detailed help on computing hardware and understanding technical jargon please refer to Chapter 9.

Advantages of the Laptop Computer

- Can be used anywhere in the home and on the move, in hotels or on the train, etc.
- Doesn't need a mains power supply (some of the time).
- Fewer cables and power points are needed.
- Takes up less room in the home — at the end of a session the laptop can be stowed away in a drawer or cupboard.

Shown below on the left is a typical laptop computer; the touch pad and buttons at the centre front replace the mouse used on desktop machines. If you prefer to use a mouse, it's quite easy to plug in a wireless or USB device, as discussed shortly.

A laptop computer with its smaller relation, the netbook

The small computer shown above on the right is one of a new generation of highly portable computers, known as *netbooks*, this particular example being an Elonex Webbook as described on the next page.

The Netbook Computer

The *netbook* is a very small laptop with a screen size of just 8 to 10 inches so that it can more easily be carried in a bag or briefcase, etc. The netbook bridges the gap between "Internet-enabled" *smartphones* (such *as* the Blackberry and the iPhone) and the conventional laptop computer.

We recently obtained an Elonex Webbook, an example of a netbook, as shown on the right of the picture on the previous page. After using the Webbook for some time I was impressed by the overall performance and quality of the machine. The Webbook is "wireless-ready" and was easily connected to the Internet via our wireless router, straight out of the box. The small screen is very clear — much better than our older full-size laptop with a bigger, 15-inch screen. The computer happily ran the Windows XP operating system pre-installed on the machine. (Many netbooks are now supplied with Windows 7.)

There is no built-in CD/DVD drive but with three USB ports (discussed in Chapter 2, Connecting the Peripherals), it's a simple matter to plug in an external drive. It's also possible to connect a full size keyboard and mouse wirelessly or via the USB ports. A VGA port enables a full-size monitor to be connected.

At around £190-£300, netbook computers provide a highly portable and cost-effective way to get onto the Internet and also carry out the full range of activities such as word processing, spreadsheets, music and e-mail. Some netbooks run the Linux operating system rather than Windows 7 or XP and may have a *solid-state drive* for storage instead of the usual hard disc drive.

Expanding a Laptop or Netbook Computer

If you're working on a laptop or netbook at home for long periods, you may want to benefit from a full-size monitor, keyboard and mouse; these can easily be connected to a laptop or netbook computer, as described in Chapter 2, Connecting the Peripherals.

Advantages of the Desktop Computer

- Usually has a better screen than a typical laptop.
- "Proper" full-size QWERTY keyboard and a mouse.
- There is plenty of room inside the desktop machine to add expansion cards and repairs are easily carried out.
- Components for a desktop computer are generally cheaper than those for the laptop machine.
- A desktop computer generally runs cooler than a laptop.
- Desktop machines have a separate keypad for entering numerical data (as do some more expensive laptops).

A desktop computer with colour laser printer

In the above computer system the base or tower unit is located underneath the work surface on a special platform in the purpose-built computer desk.

Homes With More Than One Computer

Computers are now relatively cheap and many homes may have several machines, as in my own home. There is a laptop machine which can be used anywhere in the house. Tucked away in a corner of the lounge we have a family desktop machine used mainly by my wife and myself; our son has a desktop machine in his bedroom. In the garden there is a summerhouse which has been adapted as a home office, with another desktop machine on which books like this one are produced. The machines are connected via a wireless network so they can all share a single broadband Internet connection. Wireless networks are discussed in more detail later.

Using the Laptop

The laptop machine is used mainly by my wife, in any room in the house or out in the garden on a warm day. A disadvantage is that it can only be used for a few hours before the battery needs recharging. Typical uses are browsing the Internet for information on any subject under the sun — online shopping, choosing and booking flights and holidays, solving difficult crossword clues and e-mailing electronic greetings cards containing animations, music and personal messages.

The Family Desktop Machine

In addition to browsing the World Wide Web, it's very useful to be able to print out your own bank statements, transfer money and pay bills. This computer is also used to edit and print digital photographs and send them as e-mail attachments. You can look for a second-hand car on the Auto Trader Web site or sell surplus household items on eBay. The family computer is also used for downloading music and videos and recording onto a CD or DVD. Apart from producing letters and reports on Microsoft Word and managing accounts on Excel, the computer is an excellent tool for researching your ancestry, especially since millions of census records are readily available online.

This computer has a multi-function colour inkjet printer or MFP. This cost under £40 and doubles up as a colour photocopier and scanner. There are slots on the front of the printer to allow memory cards from a digital camera to be inserted, enabling photos to be printed directly. A set of ink cartridges for this printer can be obtained for under £10 after shopping around on the Internet.

Multi-function inkjet printer

The Home Office Computer

The computer in my home office is a desktop machine, (shown on page 8), equipped with a colour laser printer; the colour printer is needed for checking the draft pages in books like this one.

Colour laser printer

Colour laser printers can be obtained for under £200. If your work doesn't require colour then monochrome laser printers are available for under £100. If you do a lot of printing, the extra speed of a laser printer will be beneficial. Toner for a laser printer may cost £50-£80. A multi-function laser printer can also be used as a photocopier and scanner.

If you only have one family computer, there can be problems; what happens if two people want to use the computer at the same time? Additionally, if your family computer is also used for work or business, it's probably not ideal to clutter your lounge with paperwork and other office paraphernalia.

The Home Office

If you're using a computer for serious purposes such as working from home, writing a novel or a parish magazine or running a small business, it's better if you can set up a separate dedicated home office. If you're fortunate enough to have a spare room, this may be ideal. It will be warm and secure and will probably already have the necessary power points. Nowadays there's no need for the room to have telephone extension cables to provide an Internet connection; if you have a telephone socket somewhere in your home, an inexpensive *wireless router* will enable several computers anywhere in the house or garden to connect to the Internet without cables.

If you don't have a spare room but still want to set up a separate home office, perhaps you have a garden with space for a suitable shed. Purpose-built home offices can be expensive but my solution was to buy a wooden summerhouse; with the addition of insulation, soundproofing and double glazing this has made a very warm, quiet office with very few distractions.

The Shed — a summerhouse used as a home office

If your home office is a shed in the garden, you really need to have a permanent power cable installed, rather than rely on temporary extension leads. This power supply should use special *armoured cable*, preferably buried at least two feet underground. The armoured cable has a metal sheath to prevent it being severed with a spade next time you, or those who come after you, are digging the garden. Even if you install the power cable yourself, it's a legal requirement to have it checked and certified as safe by a qualified electrician.

In my experience, you can't have too much desk space; perfectly good office furniture can be bought cheaply from second-hand retailers. A purpose-built computer desk with special holes for the cables and a lower platform for the base unit is a good investment for the home office. A wireless keyboard and mouse help to de-clutter the desk; the wireless mouse moves more easily than the cabled variety.

Inside the Shed — a wireless mouse and keyboard and floor-mounted tower unit ensure plenty of desk space

Working from Home

If you are retired or approaching retirement, working at home can be a rewarding and interesting way to keep yourself active; perhaps you could continue in your previous employment, possibly working fewer hours or in a consultancy capacity. Or perhaps you could write up a history of your parish or village and get it printed and published. Some people start a Web site for like-minded individuals to share helpful information.

Having taken early retirement from teaching in my fifties I was fortunate to be able to start a new career as an author working from home; thanks mainly to Michael Babani at Bernard Babani (publishing) Ltd, I have now had over 30 books published. If you've worked in a trade or profession for a good many years, perhaps there's a book in you that will allow you to pass on your experience to the younger generation. Maybe, like the vet James Herriot or the school inspector Gervase Phinn, you've amassed lots of amusing anecdotes which can be turned into a best seller.

One advantage of the separate home office in the garden is that it's a bit like going out to work, even if it's only a few yards down the garden. There's also the added bonus of not having to spend stressful hours commuting to and from work. You are away from the distractions and interruptions of your home and, if you have a partner, they get the house to themselves for a few hours. When you finish work you close the office door and leave your work behind. Working from home has the advantage that you can choose your own hours and, with fewer distractions, can be more productive. On the negative side, working for hours in a home office is a solitary activity, especially for someone used to working with other people.

Installing a Home Computer

The laptop computer doesn't need much installing since it's self-contained and only needs a single power point. However, the laptop will need to be connected to the Internet and this is discussed in Chapter 3, Getting Online.

The desktop computer will need a minimum of four power points but preferably six, to power the base unit, monitor, printer and possible additions such as a scanner, speakers and a desk light. Some extension leads have a built-in surge protector which guards against sudden "spikes" or variations in power; otherwise you can buy a separate plug-in surge protector costing about £5, which is inserted between your mains power point and the extension lead. If you live in an area where power cuts are common, a UPS (Uninterruptable Power Supply) will keep your computer powered up for long enough to shut it down correctly. (If a computer is not shut down correctly, e.g. by a sudden failure of the power supply, you are likely to lose your current work and there may be damage to other files on the computer).

The main part of the desktop computer is the *base unit*, also called the *tower unit*. This is the "engine room" of the computer and is a metal or plastic box containing all of the components discussed in Chapter 9, such as the memory, processor, motherboard and hard disc drive. The base unit may be placed on the desk alongside of the monitor although I prefer to put the base unit on the floor to save desk space. The essential items to connect are the monitor, keyboard and mouse; in addition there may be a printer and speakers. It's also necessary to connect the power cable between a power socket and the power supply unit in the back of the computer. It's best to leave the connection of the power cable until everything else has been connected.

The Monitor

The latest flat screen TFT (Thin Film Transistor) monitors give an excellent display and take up very little desk space compared with the earlier Cathode Ray Tube monitors. Some TFT monitors also contain built-in speakers. A very good 19-inch TFT monitor can be bought for under £100 with some 22-inch and 23-inch models costing under £150. Larger monitors are available but are much more expensive. (Monitors are measured diagonally across the screen.) Some monitors plug into a power point using their own cable and plug, while others have a female connection on their power cable which plugs into the power supply unit at the back of the computer. A video cable connects the monitor to the computer via a 15-pin D-type connector, shown right.

The Keyboard and Mouse

The standard way to attach the keyboard and mouse to the computer is via special cables known as *PS/2 connectors*. The cables are permanently attached to the keyboard and mouse and fit into PS/2 sockets or ports on the back of the computer. The keyboard port is normally purple while the mouse port is green. Care is needed to ensure the pins are lined up properly.

You should now be able to connect the main power cable and switch on. There will be a switch on the front of the base unit and

another on the power supply unit at the back, normally near the top, shown above to the right of **230V**. The monitor will have its own power switch on the front. The computer should now start up and after a short time display the Windows Desktop. If there is no screen display, check that all units are powered up, (indicated by green lights) and that the video cable to the monitor is firmly connected.

Shutting Down Correctly

Never end a session by switching the power off at the power point, as this may damage any files that are open.

Before shutting down the computer, save any documents or other files that you've been working on. If you have a document open in a program such as a word processor, this should be saved using **File** and **Save** from the program's menu.

Now click the Start Button at the bottom left of the screen, shown on the right, and click **Shut down**, as shown below, to close all open programs, shut down Windows and turn off the computer.

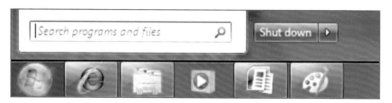

If you click the small arrow to the right of the **Shut Down** button, the small menu shown on the right appears. **Switch user** and **Log off** might be used if several people have user accounts on this computer.

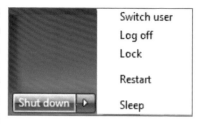

Restart shown above closes all programs, shuts down Windows and then starts the computer with Windows running again. You are often asked to **Restart** the computer in order to complete the installation of new hardware and software. The **Sleep** option (and also the **Hibernation** option used on some computers, especially laptops) puts the computer into a low power mode which saves electricity. All your work and settings are saved and later you simply press the power button to resume work where you left off.

Connecting the Peripherals

Introduction

The peripheral devices include the mouse and keyboard, printer, modem/router, flash drive, (also known as a *memory key* or *memory stick*) and speakers and headphones, etc. These devices all plug into sockets or *ports* on the case of the computer. The ports connect to the computer's motherboard. In the case of a laptop the ports are on the sides of the machine; on the desktop computer the ports are mainly on the back.

Types of Port

Most computers are fitted with several different types of port, although the USB port (discussed on page 15) is the preferred connection for many types of peripheral device.

PS/2 Ports

The green PS/2 port shown on the right is used to connect the mouse cable while the purple PS/2 port is used for the keyboard connection. USB mice and keyboards are also available; these have cables which connect to any of the USB ports on the base unit, as shown on the next page. Another option is to use a *wireless* keyboard and mouse. These are battery powered and get their signal from a small wireless "dongle", a finger-sized device which plugs into one of the USB ports.

The Serial Port

At one time these were the standard connection for mice and modems. There were often two serial ports, also known as *RS232 ports* and *communication ports*, usually referred to as COM1 and COM2. Shown on the right is a 9-pin male serial port.

The Parallel Port

Until the arrival of USB ports, this was the standard method of connecting printers and scanners. It's also known as the printer port and a Centronics port (after a manufacturer of printers). Data is transmitted in a parallel stream of bits, unlike the serial port, in which data is transmitted one bit at a time. Shown on the right is a 25-pin female parallel port.

The Ethernet Port

Although many homes now use wireless networks, businesses often prefer *cabled* networks. These are acknowledged to be faster than wireless networks but do require holes to be drilled in walls and cabling installed throughout the building. Most wired networks use a technology known as *Ethernet*; this refers to the cables, built-in network adaptors and Ethernet ports, as shown on the right. An Ethernet port and network adaptor are fitted as standard to most computers. Even on a wireless network it's often recommended that the initial setting up is done using an Ethernet cable between the router and the computer.

The Graphics VGA Port

This is the standard connection for monitors used on home and small business computers. Shown on the right is a 15-pin VGA port which accepts a standard monitor cable. These are present on laptops as well as desktop computers, allowing a separate, full size monitor to be connected to a laptop.

The Audio or Sound Ports

The audio ports shown on the right connect audio devices to the sound facilities on the motherboard or on a separate internal sound expansion card. The green port is used for sound output to speakers or headphones, pink is for input from a microphone while light blue is used for audio input, such as from an external CD drive.

USB (Universal Serial Bus) Ports

These are a relatively new type of socket and have transformed the way peripheral devices are connected. The USB ports are small rectangular slots; on a desktop computer there are  usually four USB ports at the back of the base unit and sometimes a further two at the front. Laptops usually have three or four USB ports on the side of the computer.

The USB ports can be used to connect virtually any type of peripheral device, such as:

Mouse	Keyboard
Inkjet or Laser Printer	Flash drive or memory stick
Scanner	External hard disc drive
Digital camera	Wireless adaptor
Modem	Headphones

The USB port has many advantages over the earlier serial and parallel ports, which were bulky and expensive:

- USB devices such as a digital camera, for example, can be plugged in or removed while the computer is running. This is known as "hot swapping". There's no need to shut down the computer before connecting a USB device.

- USB devices transfer data much faster than earlier technology.

- USB connections are simple and light and easy to plug in and remove.

- Some USB devices work as soon as they are plugged in, without the need for any special installation software, known as *device drivers*.

- The current USB specification in general use is USB 2.0, which is approximately ten times faster than the earlier USB 1.1, still in use on some computers. USB 2.0 is also known as Hi-Speed USB.

- If your computer only has USB 1.1 ports and you buy a USB 2.0 device, such as a flash drive, the device will still work. However you will not benefit from the extra performance of the USB 2.0 device. Similarly if a USB 2.0 device uses a connecting cable, the cable must be of the USB 2.0 standard to obtain the full performance.

- An even faster specification, called USB 3.0 or USB SuperSpeed has been developed; USB 3.0 devices are becoming available at the time of writing.

Checking Your Computer for USB 2.0 Capability

If you have a new computer it will almost certainly be equipped for USB 2.0 devices; older machines may only provide the earlier and slower USB 1.1 standard. To benefit from USB 2.0, your machine must have an **Enhanced Host Controller**, as shown highlighted in blue below; the list of USB devices is displayed after clicking **Start**, **Computer**, **System properties**, **Device manager** and double-clicking **Universal Serial Bus controllers** shown below. The word **Enhanced** below indicates that this particular computer can support USB 2.0 devices.

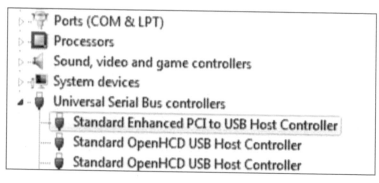

Adding Extra USB Ports

It's theoretically possible to connect 127 USB devices to a single computer, although it's hard to imagine how this might be necessary for a home computer user. However, if your computer only has 2, 3 or 4 USB ports, you may sometimes need some more. In the case of a desktop machine, there are often four USB ports on the back and two on the front. If you need to keep "hot swapping" USB devices such as USB flash drives, digital camera or headphones for example, this may be inconvenient if the ports on the back of the machine are not very accessible. You may also need to have several other USB devices permanently connected such as a printer, modem or router, wireless network adaptor "dongle" and possibly a USB keyboard and mouse.

If you are short of USB ports, a simple solution is to buy a *USB hub* typically containing 4 or 7 ports. The 4-port hub usually takes its power from the computer, whereas the larger hubs have a separate power supply cable.

A 4-port USB hub

Alternatively, you can obtain a 4-port *USB 2.0 Expansion card* which plugs into one of the PCI slots on the motherboard of a desktop computer, as discussed in Chapter 9. This provides four extra USB 2.0 ports on the back of the computer.

A 4-port USB 2.0 expansion card

Laptop users can plug a USB 2.0 4-port *PCMCIA Expansion card* into the PCMCIA slot on the side of their machine. All of these devices can typically be bought for around £10 or less.

Installing USB Devices

It's very easy to plug USB devices into the rectangular USB ports discussed earlier. Some USB devices such as flash drives and USB keyboards and mice are detected by Windows 7 and automatically installed and ready for use in seconds.

Other devices, such as USB printers, require software called *device drivers* to enable the printer to work with a particular version of Windows, such as Windows 7. A CD containing the driver software is usually supplied with the device. Some manufacturers tell you to install their drivers from the CD to your hard disc before connecting the device to the computer.

When you connect a new USB device to a computer, it is detected straightaway. Windows 7 searches for a suitable driver, if necessary searching Windows Update on the Internet. If a suitable driver is found it will be installed automatically and the new device will be ready for use very quickly, as shown below.

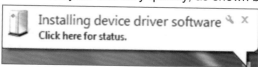

If a suitable driver is not found, Windows 7 may provide a link to the Web site of the manufacturer of the particular device.

Download and install the driver for your laser printer

Your laser printer is missing a driver.

The model name of your laser printer is Laser Shot LBP-1120.

 Click to download the new driver from the Canon Inc. website

From the manufacturer's Web site you will be able to download to your hard disc the appropriate Windows 7 driver software and complete the installation of your new device.

Methods for installing devices and drivers vary, so always read the manufacturer's instructions before starting work.

Managing Your Printer

Click the **Start** button at the bottom left of the screen and then click **Devices and Printers** from the Start Menu which appears. A window opens showing the various devices and printers attached to your computer.

It's possible to have several printers listed in the **Devices and Printers** window. In the extract above, the tick next to the **Samsung** laser printer indicates that it is the *default printer*. This computer is also set up with a driver to use a **Brother** inkjet printer as shown above. To select a different printer while using programs like Word or Excel, etc., click the small downward pointing arrow shown on the right and in the **Print** dialogue box below. Then select an alternative printer from the drop-down list, such as the **Brother** printer in the example below.

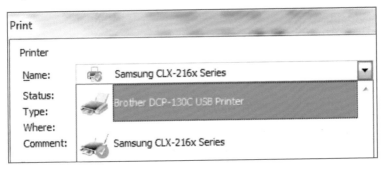

Obviously to start the printing process the printer must be connected to the computer with a USB cable and powered up.

Changing the Default Printer

In the **Devices and Printers** window shown on the previous page, a printer can be set as the default printer after right-clicking over its icon. Then select **Set as default printer** from the menu. The **Printing preferences** option shown on the right allows you to change many of the printer settings such as paper size and portrait or landscape orientation.

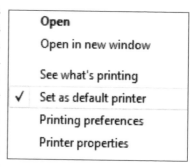

Viewing the Print Jobs

If you double-click the icon for the current printer and then select **See what's printing**, the window shown below appears.

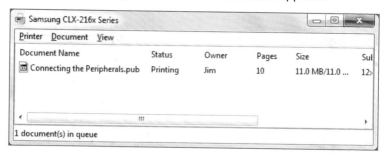

This shows the status of any current print jobs; clicking **Printer** shown on the left of the menu bar above displays a list of options including pausing and cancelling a print job. This can be useful if something goes wrong with the current printing operation, for example if you've selected the wrong pages to be printed.

Sharing a Printer

Selecting **Sharing...** on the **Printer** menu and then clicking **Change Sharing Options** allows you to switch on **Share this printer,** enabling computers on a network to share one printer.

Using a Netbook or Laptop as a Desktop

It's a simple matter to attach a bigger monitor or full-size keyboard and mouse to a laptop. (On this page the term laptop also refers to the smaller netbook machines). This might be helpful, for example, if you are doing a lot of word processing or data entry and your eyesight is not as good as it used to be. A good 19-inch TFT monitor can be bought for under £100 and this simply connects to the 15-pin D-type VGA connector on the laptop. A full-size USB keyboard and mouse can be added for about £15 or less. These plug into the USB ports on the laptop and are immediately detected and ready for use. Once the mouse, keyboard and monitor are connected, a couple of function key presses may be needed on the laptop to bring up the laptop screen display on the separate monitor. The laptop or netbook can now be used with all the ergonomic advantages of the bigger desktop machine, as shown below.

A netbook computer connected to a full-size monitor, keyboard and mouse

Jargon at a Glance

Control Panel A feature in Windows 7 which enables settings to be altered and hardware and software to be removed.

Device driver Software which enables a device to work with a particular version of Windows, such as Windows 7. A new device package should include a CD containing the driver; Windows itself and Windows Update contain drivers for many devices.

Enhanced Host Controller Hardware on the motherboard which is needed to support USB 2.0 devices.

Hot swapping Connecting or disconnecting a USB device while the computer is up and running.

Parallel port (also known as a **Centronics port**) Connection socket for earlier types of printers, etc., now superseded by USB devices.

Printers A window accessed from the Control Panel, allowing the printer settings to be altered.

Serial port A connection socket for earlier types of mouse and modem, etc. Also known as communication ports, COM1 or COM2.

USB (Universal Serial Bus) A technology for connecting peripheral devices to a computer through simple sockets or ports on the computer. USB provides much faster data transfer than earlier connection methods, such as serial or parallel ports.

USB 2.0 Also known as USB High-Speed. Currently the most widely used USB standard, much faster than the earlier USB 1.1.

USB 3.0 or USB SuperSpeed An even faster new USB design; USB 3.0 devices are becoming available at the time of writing.

USB expansion card A small circuit board containing several extra USB ports. Desktop machines use a PCI expansion card fitted internally to the computer's motherboard; laptops use a PCMCIA card which plugs into a slot in the side of the computer.

USB Hub A device which plugs into a USB port and provides several extra USB ports.

3

Getting Online

Introduction

In the last few years the Internet has become an essential part of the lives of many people and some of us probably wonder how we ever managed without it. Listed below are just a few examples of the way the Internet is used in our household:

- Ordering the weekly supermarket shopping to be delivered to our door; the total time for the entire "shop" is usually only about 10-15 minutes.
- Communicating with friends and relatives by e-mail, including photographs and electronic greetings cards.
- Checking out holiday destinations, booking flights and accommodation, checking in online for certain flights.
- Planning journeys using online maps and route planners and Google Earth to look at particular areas.
- Checking and printing bank statements, setting up standing orders and making electronic fund transfers.
- Comparing saving and investment offers.
- Buying books and other items from Amazon and other online stores, usually delivered within one or two days.
- Selling unwanted household items on eBay.
- Downloading music and software, obtaining latest *device drivers* to make computing equipment work.
- Using the RSPB Web site to identify birds from pictures, bird songs and video clips.
- Finding information on any subject using Web such as Google, Wikipedia and HowStuffWorks.

Broadband

For several years the only way home users were able to connect to the Internet was using a device called a *dial-up* modem; this linked the computer to an ordinary telephone line. In recent years a much faster system known as *broadband* has become the standard; this enables you to surf the Internet more quickly and download large files such as videos and music — painfully laborious tasks on the older and slower dial-up systems.

Most broadband services still use the BT telephone lines, but modifications must be made to your local telephone exchange before you can receive broadband. In addition the line to your home has to be *activated* by BT. You also need a special *ADSL modem* or a *router* to connect to a broadband Internet service.

Some remote areas of Britain still cannot receive broadband because their telephone exchanges have not been modified. If you already have access to an Internet computer, you can find out which broadband services are available in your area by logging on to **www.broadbandchecker.co.uk** and entering your postcode. An example of the results is shown below:

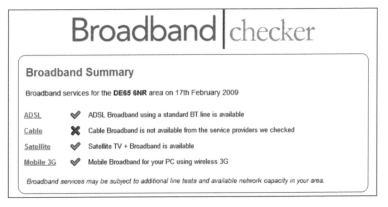

If you don't already have access to an Internet computer, you should be able to log on in a local library or Internet cafe.

Many people use the ADSL Broadband service provided by BT; some companies, such as AOL and Tiscali, deliver an Internet service over the BT phone lines. Virgin Media provide Cable Broadband to areas covered by cable television and Sky offer TV and Broadband via satellite. Some mobile phone companies provide an Internet connection using a modem which plugs into a USB port on your computer. In some remote areas where ADSL lines are not available, a *wireless* broadband service is provided.

Internet Service Providers

There is a bewildering number of Internet Service Providers but, if you already have access to the Internet, you can look at several Web sites comparing the various offers from the ISPs. These comparisons cover such details as the monthly cost (anything from £7 to £25) and the maximum download speed (currently 8Mbps is common). (Please see Chapter 9 for an explanation of Mbps or megabits per second). Most Internet service providers will tie you into a minimum contract time, typically 12 or 18 months. Some Internet Service Providers include a free router valued at about £50 and may also provide the cables and filters and software to complete your setup. Shown below is an extract from the Broadband-Finder Web site (**www.broadband-finder.co.uk**). This site also includes an option to enter your postcode and find all the services available in your area.

Provider	Package	Usage	Speed	Download Limit	Setup Cost	Contract Period	Monthly Cost	1st Year Cost **
BT	Online Exclusive: BT Broadband - Option 1 FREE new Wireless Black BT Home Hub available with £20 off your bill with Option 1. Option 1 now comes with 8Mbps download speed and a 10GB monthly download limit. Order online now or call free on 0800 328 1522. More >	LIGHT	Up To 8Mbps	10GB	FREE	18 Months	£7.78	£164.18
	Recommended: TalkTalk Broadband - Essentials Create your personalised broadband package with TalkTalk 'Essentials', the new broadband package from TalkTalk. Also includes a FREE wireless router. Order online or call 0800 049 7842 to order over the	MEDIUM	Up To 8Mbps	40GB	£29.99	18 Months	£6.49	£107.87

Broadband Requirements

The next few pages explain how to set up a computer to use an ADSL broadband service based on the BT telephone lines. The essential requirements are:

- An account with an Internet Service Provider such as BT, AOL or Tiscali, etc.

- A BT telephone socket and a telephone line which has been tested by BT and activated for ADSL broadband.

- An ADSL modem or a *router* containing an ADSL modem. Many Internet Service Providers now include a free router as part of the package.

- One or more *filters* allowing a telephone socket to be used for broadband and phone calls at the same time .

- A cable to connect the modem or router to the filter.

- An Ethernet cable to assist in the initial setup of the router to the computer.

- A *network adaptor* in each desktop machine connected to the Internet. This may be in the form of a PCI expansion card fitted inside of the computer; alternatively the adaptor can be a "dongle" which plugs into a USB port on the computer. Laptop computers normally have built-in wireless networking capability.

- Software and instructions for setting up the modem or router, usually on a CD included in the startup package from the Internet Service Provider, such as BT.

- In the case of a wireless router, a *network name* and a *security key* to prevent other people from logging on to your Internet connection from outside of your home. (Wireless home networks may have a range of 100-300 feet, depending on obstructions like walls and floors.)

The Wireless Router

A wireless router with a built-in ADSL modem is one of the most popular ways of connecting to the Internet. Many Internet Service Providers include a free router in their startup kit. A wireless router will be fine even if you only have one computer; if you have more than one computer, the wireless router will allow them all to be connected to the Internet simultaneously using a single telephone socket.

The wireless network is a good solution for most home users since it avoids the alternative system of drilling holes in walls, etc., and trailing Ethernet cables all round the house or flat. I have found wireless technology to be extremely reliable using computers scattered about the house in different rooms, requiring the wireless signals to pass through several walls.

The initial setting up of the router may require a computer to be sitting next to the router and connected to it by an Ethernet networking cable. However, once the network is up and running the wireless router can sit on its own next to your telephone socket, with no computers physically connected to it by Ethernet cables. In the example below, our router is placed in the dining room next to the telephone socket, while the computers themselves are in different rooms around the house.

A BT Home Hub router sits almost unobtrusively in the dining room

The Wireless Router Startup Kit

If you subscribe to an Internet Service Provider such as BT, you may obtain a free wireless router and the various components needed to get you started, as shown below.

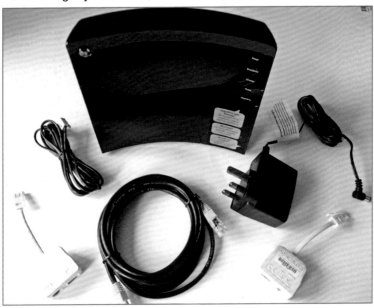

The BT Home Hub wireless router and accessories

In the above photograph, the router itself is the large black box at the rear. On the right is the power supply cable and transformer. The white cables and sockets are known as *filters* or *microfilters*; these plug into the main telephone socket(s) in your home. Each filter itself has two sockets; one socket connects an ordinary telephone handset while the other connects the broadband cable from the router. This is the black cable shown to the left of the router above. The filter enables an ordinary telephone to be used at the same time as the broadband Internet.

The black cable with yellow ends shown above is an Ethernet cable, which may be needed in the initial setting up of the router.

The Router Ports in Detail

Shown below are ports on the rear of the wireless router supplied by BT as part of their broadband package.

The ports on the back of the BT Home Hub wireless router

The left-hand socket in the group above is used for the cable which connects the router to the broadband telephone socket, via a filter, as mentioned on the previous page. The green socket is for a special BT Internet telephone. The four yellow Ethernet sockets have several uses, such as the initial setting up of the router using an Ethernet cable connected to a computer. The Ethernet sockets can also be used to create a *wired network,* using Ethernet cables and adaptors instead of wireless technology. Wired networks are often preferred in business, since they can be faster than wireless and unsightly cables may not be such an issue as they are in a home environment.

On the right of the router above is the socket for the power cable; finally there is a USB socket to connect a USB cable to a USB port on a computer (as an alternative to an Ethernet cable.)

BT Vision

One of the Ethernet sockets on the router can be used to connect an Ethernet cable from the router to a BT Vision digital television box. This allows a large number of Freeview programs to be viewed and recorded; live television can be paused and restarted. A daily program guide can be downloaded and extra programs and films are available on demand, (for a fee).

Instruction Manuals

The router package should also include an instruction manual and a quick-start leaflet; increasingly a more comprehensive instruction manual is being provided on the CD which normally accompanies the router.

Wireless Network Adaptors

Each computer on a wireless network must be equipped with electronic components to enable the computer to detect and communicate with the wireless router. Modern laptop computers are normally supplied with wireless networking capability already built in, although this may need to be switched on.

USB Wireless Network Adaptors

Desktop computers may need to be fitted with a separate *wireless network adaptor*. This may take the form of a "dongle" which plugs into a USB port on the computer. A cable allows the USB network adaptor to be moved about to obtain the best wireless signal.

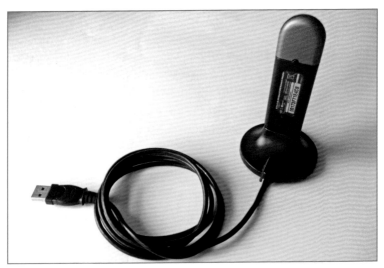

A USB wireless network adaptor

PCI Wireless Network Adaptors

The PCI wireless network adaptor fits inside the cover of the base unit of a desktop computer; it's a simple job to unscrew the cover of the base unit and press the adaptor into a vacant PCI slot on the computer's motherboard, as discussed in Chapter 9.

A wireless network adaptor in the form of a PCI expansion card

A network adaptor may be included in a wireless router package. Otherwise they can be purchased for under £10 from computer shops and by mail order. The package should also include installation instructions and a CD containing the driver software.

802.11 Wireless Protocols

Wireless (or Wi-Fi) equipment such as routers and network adaptors must conform to various *protocols* or technical specifications. Currently most wi-fi equipment is specified as **802.11b**, **802.11g** or the latest protocol, **802.11n**. Check with the router manual to find the **802.11** adaptor specification compatible with your router.

Installing a Wireless Network

Before you can start to set up a wireless network based on a wireless router, your telephone line must be tested and activated for ADSL broadband by BT. If you are using an Internet Service Provider other than BT, they may make the arrangements for you. You might have to wait a week or 10 days for the activation to be effective.

Once the telephone line is activated you can start installing the router. Ideally the router should be in a central position in your home if you are connecting several computers. If possible, avoiding installing the router near to a microwave oven or cordless phones as these may interfere with the broadband.

Place a filter in the main telephone socket in your home. If you want to use an ordinary telephone here, there is a socket for this on the filter. Now connect the special broadband cable (known as an RJ11 cable) from the router to the other socket in the filter. (The broadband and ordinary telephone sockets in the filter are quite different, so you can't connect the cables incorrectly.)

Now connect the power cable from a power point to the router and switch on. Initially the diagnostic lights on the front of the router will flash yellow and then after a minute or two the power, broadband and wireless lights should be constant blue.

Set up a computer within a few feet of the router. This computer should be fitted with a wireless network adaptor as discussed earlier. Most modern laptops have built-in wireless networking capability although this may need to be switched on. Some desktop computers are also "wireless ready" but otherwise they need a USB or PCI wireless adaptor fitted, as discussed earlier. BT provide an installation CD which is intended to be used on every computer, although this is not essential to make the connection to the Internet.

Start up the computer and the small Internet icon shown on the right will initially display a yellow star; hover the cursor  over this icon and it should display the message **Connections are available**, as shown above. Click the Internet icon and a list of nearby wireless networks is displayed, including yours, as shown below:

In the above example, three networks have been detected; the name of a network such as **BTHomeHub-5778** is also referred to as the *SSID* or *Service Set Identifier*. Now click the name of your router, such as the **BTHomeHub** and then click the **Connect** button. You must then enter a *wireless key* to make the network secure. The BT security key is displayed on the back of the router and on a small card provided in the router package.

Entering the Security Key

The security key or password must be entered into every computer the first time it is connected to the router. If you don't have a secure network, any of your neighbours or someone nearby with a laptop could use your Internet connection and possibly hack into your data.

The dialogue box for entering the security key is shown below.

All being well, once you click **Connect** you will be told that you are successfully connected to the router and the Internet. This is also indicated by the Internet icon shown on the right in the Notification Area of the Taskbar at the bottom right of the screen. If you hover the cursor over this icon it should give the name of the wireless hub and confirm that you have *Internet Access*, as shown below.

Using an Ethernet Cable to Connect a Router

An Ethernet cable, also known as an RJ45 cable, usually with yellow connectors at each end, should be supplied with your router kit. If you are unable, for any reason, to make a wireless connection to the Internet, the Ethernet cable provides a temporary direct link between your router and the computer.

Some routers, such as those made by Belkin and Linksys, require you to connect the computer with an Ethernet cable; then, using a Web browser such as Internet Explorer, type the *IP address* of the router, such as **192.168.2.1** for example, into the browser's address bar, as shown below.

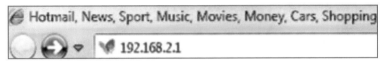

This IP address will connect you to the router in the same way that an IP address can be used to connect to a Web page. You can now set up the router using settings provided by your Internet Service Provider. These might include a username and password and other details such as the type of wireless security, usually either WEP or WPA. These are methods of *encryption* which involves encoding information so that only people with a key can *decipher* it. Please see your router's instruction manual for the precise details for creating a secure network.

Once the router and each computer are set up, you can dispense with the Ethernet cables and connect to the Internet wirelessly.

With the BT Home Hub router discussed earlier it should not be necessary to connect the computer to the router using an Ethernet cable. This is because the BT Home Hub is already set up and often only requires the wireless key to be entered to make the connection. However, should there be any problems in connecting wirelessly, it might be helpful to plug in the Ethernet cable, connect to the Internet and login to your Internet Service Provider's Web site or router manufacturer to obtain online help.

Checking Your Internet Connection

Right-click the Internet icon at the bottom right of the screen, then from the menu which pops up click **Open Network and Sharing Center**. This dialogue box allows you to view many aspects of your new wireless network. You can also set up your network so that files, printers and other resources can be shared by all of the computers on the network.

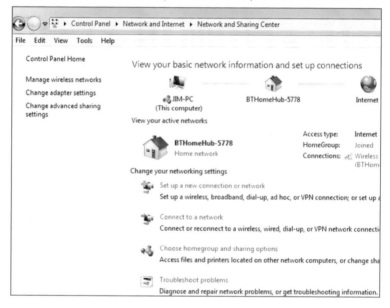

You can also check the speed of your broadband Internet connection. At the time of writing, many services offer a download speed of up to 10Mbps and a few offer up to 24Mbps. In practice this speed may not be achieved due to limitations such as your distance from the telephone exchange. You can check your speeds by logging onto a Web site such as:

www.broadbandspeedchecker.co.uk

Now follow the instructions on the screen to test the upload and download speeds of your broadband connection.

Summary: Getting Online

The following list outlines the general method of connecting to the Internet using a BT ADSL broadband telephone line and a wireless router:

1. Check that you can receive ADSL broadband from your local telephone exchange.

2. Sign up with an Internet Service Provider.

3. Wait for BT to test and activate your telephone line to receive broadband.

4. Obtain a wireless router with a built-in ADSL modem. Your Internet Service Provider may supply this.

5. Insert a microfilter into the main telephone socket in your home.

6. Insert the cable from a telephone handset into the telephone socket in the microfilter.

7. Connect the broadband cable from the router into the broadband socket in the microfilter.

8. Connect the power lead for the router and switch on. The power light on the router should be on; then the wireless and broadband lights should stop flashing.

9. Set up a "wireless enabled" computer near to the router. If necessary attach an RJ45 Ethernet cable between the router and the computer.

10. Start up the computer and connect to the Internet using a Web browser such as Internet Explorer. Enter the wireless key and/or any other information for your router or supplied by your Internet Service Provider.

11. Remove the Ethernet cable and repeat steps 9 and 10 for any other computers on the network.

12. You should now be able to connect wirelessly to the Internet from any computer on the network.

Jargon at a Glance

Activation BT test and prepare your broadband Internet telephone line so that it's ready for use on the *activation date*.

ADSL (Asymmetric Digital Subscriber Line) Technology which transmits broadband data over copper telephone lines.

Broadband Very fast transfer of data and information over the Internet via ADSL telephone lines, cable, satellite and wireless, etc.

Encryption A method of "scrambling" wireless data so that it can't easily be decoded by a "hacker". WEP is an earlier form of coding while WPA is a later, more secure system.

Ethernet Cables, adaptors and ports used to connect devices using wires known as RJ45 cables.

Filter or microfilter A connector allowing broadband and an ordinary telephone to share a telephone socket simultaneously.

Google Internet "search engine" allowing you to type in keywords to find information on any subject, also images, maps and news.

IP Address (Internet Protocol) A numeric string, e.g. **198.168.2.1** which uniquely identifies a computer or device on the Internet, similar to a Web address such as **www.babanibooks.com**.

ISP (Internet Service Provider) Company charging users a subscription to connect to the Internet via their *server* computers.

Modem Device for converting computer data for transmission over telephone lines. Broadband usually requires an ADSL modem or a *router* with a built-in ADSL modem.

Network adaptor A device connecting a computer to a local area network. May be an internal PCI card or external USB "dongle".

Router Device allowing several computers to share a single Internet connection and share files and printers, wirelessly or with cables.

Wireless (Wi-Fi) protocol Technical specification used to define standards of wireless equipment, such as **802.11b**, **g**, or **n**.

Wireless key Password used to prevent unauthorised access to a wireless router.

Exploring the Internet and E-mail

Introduction

The Internet is a worldwide network of millions of computers known as *servers*; the servers store billions of pages of information, making up the World Wide Web. Internet Explorer is known as a *Web browser*, a program designed to help you find and display Web pages on a particular subject. Internet Explorer connects to Web servers anywhere in the world which hold the information you require. Then the Web pages are *downloaded* to your own computer, which is known as a *network client* as opposed to a *network server*.

Internet Explorer can be launched by clicking the **Start** button at the bottom left of the desktop and selecting **Internet Explorer** from the top of the Start Menu.

Your Home Page

Clicking **Internet Explorer** above connects you to the Internet and opens the Web page which has been set up as your Home Page. There may be a key on your keyboard, usually marked with an icon for a house, taking you straight to your Home Page with a single press. You can change your Home Page in Internet Explorer after selecting **Tools** and **Internet Options**.

Searching for Information

The MSN UK Home Page has a Search Bar into which you type keywords which precisely identify the subject you are interested in, such as "**the red squirrel**", for example, as shown below.

When you click the magnifying glass icon shown on the right above, a list of Web sites appears as shown below; these contain your keywords somewhere within their pages.

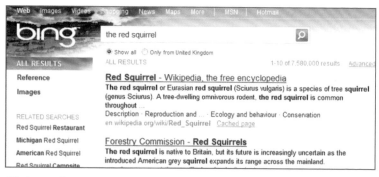

Click on the underlined blue links above to download the Web pages from the Internet and view them on your computer. Sites near the top of the list are usually the most relevant.

Please note in the above list of search results there is one result which pops up near the top of many searches; this is **Wikipedia**, a free, online encyclopedia which anyone can edit.

You can concentrate your search on various categories such as **News**, **Maps** and **Images**, etc., by clicking the category name as shown in the MSN Search Bar at the top of this page.

By default the actual searching in Internet Explorer is done by a *search engine* called Bing. This is Microsoft's rival to Google, currently the world's most popular program for searching the Net.

Google

A search engine is a computer program designed to find information from the Internet. Although you will probably find searching using the Bing search engine in MSN perfectly satisfactory, Google has established itself as the world leader. Google is free and can be obtained after entering **www.google.co.uk** into the Address Bar at the top of your Web browser, such as Internet Explorer, as shown below.

The Google page opens with the blank Search Bar ready to accept your keyword searches, as shown below.

You can focus your search on categories such as **News**, **Images** and **Maps,** etc. **Google Maps** and **Google Earth** (a separate free program) allow you to see maps and satellite images of places all over the world. **Street View** shows actual photographs of buildings, cars and people. Right-click over the Google window shown above and select **Create Shortcut** and **Yes** to place a clickable icon for Google on your Windows desktop.

Browsing the World Wide Web

When you are connected to a Web site you can move to other Web pages and other Web sites using *clickable links* or *hyperlinks.* As you move the cursor around the screen, when it's over a clickable link the cursor changes to a hand. The link may be a piece of text, a picture or an icon. A text link appears underlined while the cursor is over it, as shown by the **Hotmail** link on the right. In this example, a single click of the link takes you from the MSN Home Page to the Microsoft Hotmail, a Web-based e-mail service.

As you move about the Web using clickable links to visit various pages, you may wish to move between pages previously visited. This is achieved by clicking the forward and back buttons found near the top left of the Internet Explorer screen and shown on the right and below.

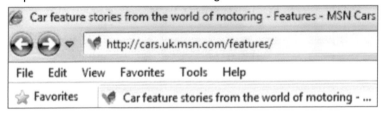

The **File** menu above includes options to **Save** and **Print** a Web page. Clicking **View** above displays options to switch various toolbars on or off, including the Menu Bar itself (**File**, **Edit**, **View**, etc.,) and to increase the size of the text on the screen. The **Tools** menu allows you to block *pop-ups* — unsolicited advertisements which can be very annoying when they suddenly appear on the screen. The **Tools** menu also allows you to change your Home Page, i.e. the Web page which automatically appears when you connect to the Internet at the start of a session.

The tab along the bottom right of the screenshot above starting **Car feature stories...** gives details of the current Web page.

Tabbed Browsing

Later versions of Internet Explorer allow you to have several Web sites open simultaneously, represented by tabs across the top of the screen. To switch between Web sites you simply click the tab representing the required Web site.

The group of icons shown below appears near the top right of the Internet Explorer screen.

Reading from left to right, clicking the house icon returns you to your Home Page. The next icon, when coloured orange, represents *RSS feeds*; these are regularly updated items of news and information, relevant to the currently open Web page. The printer icon allows you to print the current Web page on paper and **Page** includes options to save, copy and e-mail a Web page. The **Tools** menu above is very similar to the **Tools** menu on the Menu Bar described on the previous page.

Bookmarking Web Sites

The **Favorites** menu on the previous page and the **Favorites Center** shown below, allow you to bookmark a Web site for future use. To add a Web site to your list of favourite sites, click the overlapping yellow icons shown on the right, then select **Add to Favorites....**

To revisit a site, open **Favorites** and click the name of the site, such as **Horse Riding Centres** shown on the right. The **History** feature shown on the right works in a similar way, allowing you to connect to a Web site from a list of sites which you have visited recently.

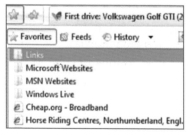

Entering Web Addresses

So far we have looked at finding Web pages by searching for relevant keywords such as **American crayfish**, for example. However, you are often given the unique address of a Web site in an advertisement or on headed paper, etc. Most British Web addresses are something like:

www.babanibooks.com

In the above example, **.com** may be replaced by, for example, **.co.uk**, **.net**, or **.org**, depending on the type of organisation owning the Web site. The Web address, such as **www.babanibooks.com**, is entered into the Address Bar of your Web browser, as shown below in Internet Explorer.

When you press **Enter**, the characters **http://** are added automatically to complete the full Web address. The required Web site then opens displaying its Home Page.

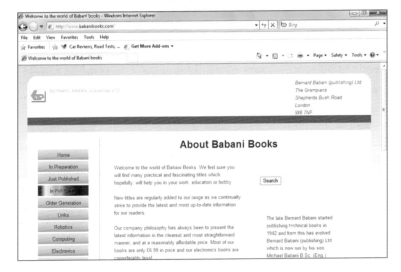

Alternative Web Browsers

This chapter has been based on Internet Explorer 8, the Web browser supplied as part of Windows 7 and currently the most popular program for surfing the Net. However, after complaints from at least one other browser company, Microsoft agreed to offer a choice of alternative browsers. These can be downloaded from a Browser Choice window as shown below.

The choice window is displayed if you are currently using Internet Explorer as your Web browser and automatic updates are turned on in Windows Update (as discussed in Chapter 8). Before the Browser Choice window opens, a note appears explaining the choice you are about to be given and that the Internet Explorer icon will be unpinned from the Taskbar. Click **OK** to open the Browser Choice window as shown below.

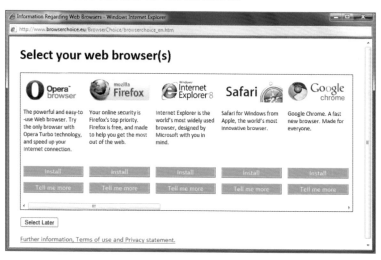

A description of each browser is displayed by clicking **Tell me more**, as shown above. Click **Install** and **Run** to set up one of the above Web browsers on your computer. Internet Explorer will still be available from the Start/All Programs menu and can be pinned back on the Taskbar if desired.

Keeping in Touch with Windows Live Mail

E-mail is a fast and easy method of communication between people anywhere in the world. Many e-mails are just a paragraph or two of text but they can also have longer documents and pictures "clipped" on as *attachments.* Earlier versions of Microsoft Windows contained their own software for preparing, sending and reading e-mails; Windows 7 does not contain its own e-mail software but you can easily download the latest Microsoft e-mail program from the Internet. This is called Windows Live Mail and is part of a suite of free, downloadable Microsoft programs known as Windows Live Essentials.

Downloading Windows Live Essentials

You can download Windows Live Essentials, after typing the following address into the Address Bar in Internet Explorer.

http://download/live.com/

Click the **Download** button which appears on the right of the screen. It's then just a case of following the on-screen instructions. You are given a chance to choose some or all of the programs which make up the Windows Live Essentials suite. Make sure **Mail** is ticked as shown below then click **Install**.

Choose the programs you want to install

Click each program name for details.

		Mail
☑ 👥 Messenger		With Windows Live Mail on your desktop, you can
☑ 📓 Mail		access multiple e-mail accounts in one program,
☑ 🖼 Photo Gallery		plus your calendar, newsgroups, and feeds. And

Launching Windows Live Mail

Click the Start Button and then select **Windows Live Mail** from the Start Menu or from the **Windows Live** menu, within the **All Programs** menu, as shown on the right.

Windows Live
→ Windows Live Call
🔒 Windows Live Family Safety
📓 Windows Live Mail
👥 Windows Live Messenger
🎬 Windows Live Movie Maker
🖼 Windows Live Photo Gallery

Before using the program for the first time you need to obtain an e-mail address and password from the provider of your e-mail service, such as BT or TalkTalk, for example. Two of the main types of e-mail service are called Hotmail and POP3.

Creating a Hotmail Account

Hotmail is a Web-based service and is simple to set up and use. All you need is a unique e-mail address and a password.

Common types of e-mail address are as follows:

stella@aol.com

james@msn.com

enquiries@wildlife.org.uk

Click **Add e-mail account** as shown at the bottom of the **Inbox** window on page 48 to open the **Add an E-mail Account** window. Enter your e-mail address and password, followed by your chosen **Display Name**, which will appear at the top of any messages you send. Click **Next** to complete the new account.

Creating a POP3 E-mail Account

POP3 services use special computers known as *mail servers* to handle e-mail. When you enter the e-mail address and password for a new e-mail account, Windows Live Mail may automatically detect the details of your e-mail service. If not, click the box next to **Manually configure server settings....** Then enter the details of the mail servers provided by your e-mail service provider. Shown below is some sample e-mail information from BT.

E-mail address:	johnsmith@btinternet.com
Username:	johnsmith
Password:	********
POP3 Incoming mail server:	mail.btinternet.com
SMTP Outgoing mail server:	mail.btinternet.com

Using Windows Live Mail

Launch the program from the Start Menu or by clicking **All Programs** then **Windows Live** and **Windows Live Mail**. Make sure **Mail** is selected at the bottom left of the screen.

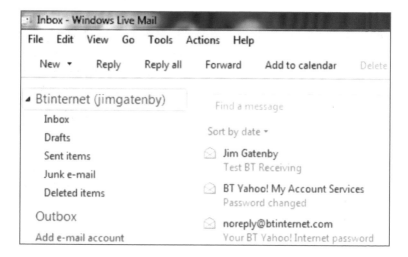

Creating a New Message

Click **New** on the left of the Toolbar near the top of the screen as shown above. The **New Message** window opens as shown below. First enter the e-mail addresses of all of the intended recipients in the **To:** bar shown below, separating multiple addresses with commas or semi-colons.

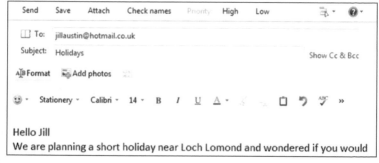

Entering the Text

After entering a title for the e-mail in the **Subject:** bar, the text is typed into the main body of the **New Message** window as shown on the previous page. The appearance of an e-mail can be enhanced with various formatting tools as discussed on page 52.

Sending an E-mail

When the e-mail is finished click the **Send** button on the Toolbar at the top left of the screen. The message will be available to the recipients when they next read their mail. If the message has been successfully sent, it will be listed in your **Sent items** folder.

Receiving an E-mail

Open **Windows Live Mail** and if necessary click **Inbox** to reveal the list of messages in the centre pane. Any unread mail is marked by a yellow icon in the shape of an unopened envelope. Double-click an e-mail in the list to open up the message. **Reply** shown below makes it easy to send a response back to the sender of an e-mail and **Reply all** sends the response to all recipients of the original e-mail; **Forward** is used to send the message on to someone else.

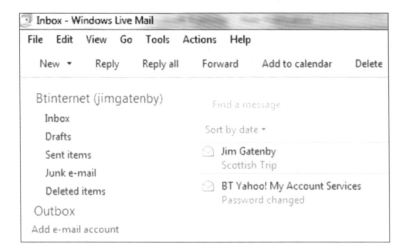

Adding an Attachment to an E-mail

It's possible to send one or more files "clipped" to an e-mail; these files are known as *attachments* and might be photos, word processing documents, or Excel spreadsheets, for example.

During the creation of a new message, perhaps when you've completed the text, click **Attach** from the Toolbar near the top left of the new e-mail window, shown below.

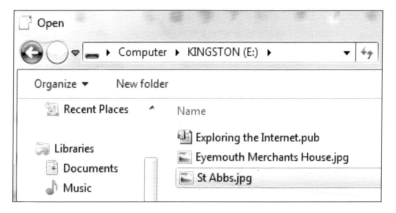

The **Open** window appears as shown below, allowing you to browse on your computer and select the required photo or document file, etc. This will probably be stored on your computer's hard disc, usually the **(C:)** drive. However, in this example I have selected a photograph, **St Abbs.jpg**, stored on a removable *flash drive* called **KINGSTON**, designated drive **E:**.

Having selected the required file, click the **Open** button at the bottom of the **Open** window. After a few seconds the name of the attached file appears under the 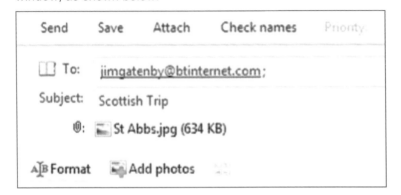 **Subject** bar on the New Message window, as shown below.

📎: ▦ St Abbs.jpg (634 KB)

Send	Save	Attach	Check names	Priority

▢ To: jimgatenby@btinternet.com;

Subject: Scottish Trip

📎: ▦ St Abbs.jpg (634 KB)

A̱B Format   🖼 Add photos

Opening an Attachment

When you click the **Send** button the message is delivered to the intended recipients together with any attachments. When your contacts read the message the attachment appears near the top. An attached picture is also displayed in the text area of the message.

Reply	Reply all	Forward	Add to calendar	Delete	Junk	Print

Jim Gatenby

To: jimgatenby@btinternet.com;

📎 ▦ St Abbs.jpg (650 KB)

The attachment is opened for viewing in its *associated program* by double-clicking its name. For example, a picture might open in Windows Photo Viewer, a spreadsheet in Microsoft Excel. Now the attached file can be viewed, saved or printed on paper.

You can test that your e-mail is working correctly by sending a message to your own e-mail address.

Enhancing a Message

The **New Message** window shown at the bottom of page 48 has a range of tools for changing the appearance of a message.

The Formatting Toolbar shown above has many of the text effects found in a word processor, such as different fonts or styles of lettering. You can change the colour of the text and also the background colour. To see the function of any of the icons on the Formatting Toolbar, select a piece of text that you have entered then allow the cursor to hover over the icon.

Clicking the small face icon on the right of the toolbar displays an array of *emoticons*; these are different facial expressions which  can be inserted into a message to express various feelings.

Stationery presents a large choice of elaborate designs which can be used as a background "wallpaper" for a message.

The icon shown on the right and on the extreme right of the Formatting Toolbar shown above allows you to insert into an e-mail message a live link to a Web site. When someone reads your e-mail they simply click the link to connect to the Internet and view a Web site you think will interest them.

Add photos shown on the right and on the Formatting Toolbar above opens a window to  allow you to search your computer's hard disc, etc., for suitable photographs to insert into the text of your message. Various borders can be added to the photos.

Large photographs take a long time to upload and send; you can alter the size of an image using the settings shown on the right, which appear when the photo is selected in the **New Message** window.

5

Windows 7 Revealed

Introduction

Early computers were controlled by entering words like **RUN**, **SAVE** and **PRINT** at the keyboard. These text-based systems were laborious and difficult to use. In the early 1980s the Xerox and Apple companies developed the *Graphical User Interface,* a system of controlling a computer by "pointing and clicking" objects on the screen using a device we now know as a *mouse.* The screen objects included *icons,* i.e. small pictures representing tasks such as starting a new page, opening a document to read on the screen, saving a document as a file on disc or printing on paper, as shown on the right. There were also lists of options or *menus* which popped down on the screen from horizontal menu bars. Information was entered and displayed on the screen in rectangular boxes known as *windows.*

The Apple Macintosh was the first computer to exploit this easy-to-use new system for operating a computer, after which Microsoft developed its own graphical user interface, known as *Windows,* in 1985. There have been several versions of Windows since then and nowadays the majority of new desktop and laptop computers are supplied with Microsoft Windows already installed. This book is based on the latest version of Windows, known as Windows 7, which is proving to be very popular and easy to use.

Microsoft Windows is by far the most commonly used software to control a computer although the Apple Mac and Linux operating systems also have many devoted users.

The Evolution of Windows 7

Before the launch of Windows 7, most new computers for the home user were supplied with either Windows XP or Windows Vista. Windows XP was released in 2001 and has proved very popular and reliable. Windows Vista was introduced in 2007 and brought in many radical new features such as Windows Aero 3D graphics shown below. (Windows Aero graphics are also included in Windows 7).

These Vista graphics features demand more computing power. While most new computers could run Windows Vista, some older machines did not have the necessary power. It was necessary for some users to upgrade their machines with more powerful components such as extra memory and a better graphics card to control the screen display. The other alternative for anyone wanting to run Vista was to buy a completely new computer. Not surprisingly, many users decided to stay with Windows XP rather than upgrade to Vista. As discussed on the next page, Windows 7 overcomes many of the criticisms of Windows Vista.

Advantages of Windows 7

This version of Microsoft Windows has been developed after taking into account feedback from users, based on their experience with earlier versions such as Windows XP and Vista. As a result, Windows 7 addresses many of the shortcomings of the earlier operating systems and has been greeted with critical acclaim. Some of the advantages of Windows 7, compared with Windows Vista and earlier systems are:

- The screen layout is simpler, less cluttered and with larger icons. The general design is more stylish.
- Searching for documents and other files is faster.
- The user can tailor Windows 7 to match their needs, so that frequently-used programs can be launched easily.
- The computer starts up and shuts down faster.
- Tests using the same computer have shown that Windows 7 performs many tasks faster than Vista.
- Windows 7 requires a less powerful computer than Vista and can even be used with tiny *netbook* computers.
- Windows 7 has been found to work well with older designs of software and hardware such as printers. In the past, new operating systems have often been incompatible with older equipment because essential new software *drivers* were not available.
- Sharing files across several computers in a home network has been simplified.
- Windows 7 supports *touch-screen* operation. (This requires a special monitor or screen.)
- Users of Windows 7 have a choice of freely-downloadable *Web browsers* as an alternative to Internet Explorer, such as the popular Mozilla Firefox.

Functions of the Windows 7 Operating System

Some of the main tasks carried out by the Windows 7 operating system are:

- Starting up and shutting down the computer.
- Controlling the screen display of windows, icons, etc.
- Managing the saving and printing of documents as *files*.
- Installing, running and removing *applications,* i.e. programs used for tasks such as word processing, drawing, spreadsheets and editing photographs.
- Installing, setting up and removing hardware such as printers and network devices like modems, routers, etc.
- Carrying out "housekeeping" tasks such as deleting files, preparing and maintaining the hard disc drive.
- Managing connections to networks such as a small home or local area network (LAN) and the Internet.
- Tailoring a computer, through the Ease of Access Center, to help someone with *special needs*, such as impaired vision or reduced manual dexterity.
- Providing security software, such as *Windows Firewall*, to prevent hackers from accessing the computer.
- Downloading the latest software updates, from Microsoft via the Internet, e.g. for improved security.
- Providing online help and support.

The following pages describe some of the new features in Windows 7, designed to make computers easier to use. These include a redesigned Taskbar with large icons enabling frequently used programs to be launched easily. Also Jump Lists which provide a quick way to return to documents you've been working on or to revisit Web sites you've looked at recently.

The Desktop in Detail

After the computer starts up, you are presented with the Windows Desktop, as shown below.

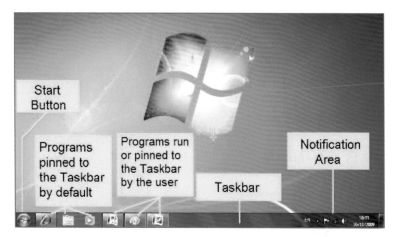

Start Button

Programs pinned to the Taskbar by default

Programs run or pinned to the Taskbar by the user

Taskbar

Notification Area

The Taskbar shown across the bottom of the screen above is the starting point for most computing sessions; for example, to start a word processing session you would load a program such as Microsoft Word. Launching a program can be done using various methods, as follows:

• Click the name of the program in the Start Menu.

• Click the name of the program in the All Programs Menu.

• Click an icon for the program on the Windows 7 Taskbar.

(As discussed shortly, you can add or remove programs listed on the Start Menu. Icons for launching programs can also be added to or removed from the Windows 7 Taskbar.)

The Start Menu

This is launched by clicking the Start Button at the bottom left of the screen. The items listed in the left-hand panel are programs that are used frequently.

The programs listed on the Start Menu on the previous page include Windows 7 **Accessories** such as **Windows Media Center** and **Calculator**. Other software, such as **Word 2010** and **Excel 2010** must be bought and installed as part of Office 2010. **Publisher 2010** is available separately. You can add programs to the Start Menu and also remove them, as discussed shortly. The items listed on the right of the Start Menu shown on the previous page are shortcuts to important features such as **Computer**, **Control Panel** and **Devices and Printers**. These features are used for managing and setting up the computer.

Shutting Down

At the bottom right of the Start Menu is the **Shut down** button; shutting down should be done correctly to avoid damaging your files and this is discussed in more detail on page 12.

The All Programs Menu

This is a large collection of menus and sub-menus. It is launched by clicking **All Programs**, shown at the bottom of the Start Menu on the previous page. Shown on the right is the **Accessories** sub-menu in the **All Programs** menu. The other installed programs can be revealed using the vertical scroll bar shown on the right.

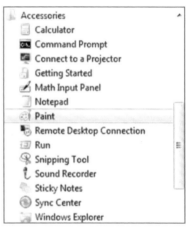

Some of the programs listed in the All Programs Menu will be used rarely or not at all; frequently used programs can be launched more quickly and easily after adding them to the Start Menu. Programs in regular use can also be launched with a single click from icons created on the Windows Taskbar, as discussed on the next page.

Launching Programs from the Taskbar

Any program can be launched by clicking its icon in the All Programs Menu. However, if you use a program regularly, this is not the quickest method. For example, I use Microsoft Publisher a great deal. Windows 7 allows you to permanently "pin" an icon for a program onto the Taskbar at the bottom of the screen.

Pinning an Icon to the Taskbar or Start Menu

Select **Start**, **All Programs** and right-click over the program's name in the All Programs Menu. Then select **Pin to Taskbar** or **Pin to Start Menu** as shown on the

Open
Troubleshoot compatibility
Pin to Taskbar
Pin to Start Menu

right. In the example below, the icon for Microsoft Publisher has been pinned to the Taskbar.

With a program pinned to the Taskbar, it can be launched very quickly with a single click; when a program is currently running, its Taskbar icon is surrounded by a highlighted rectangle, as shown on the right.

If you launch a program from the Start Menu or the All Programs Menu, an icon for the program will appear on the Taskbar, surrounded by a rectangle, but will disappear when you close the program. To make a Taskbar icon permanent, right-click the icon and select **Pin this program to taskbar**. A pinned icon will stay on the Taskbar until you remove it by right-clicking the icon and clicking **Unpin this program from taskbar**.

To remove a program from the Start Menu, right-click the name of the program and select **Unpin from Start Menu**.

Default Taskbar Icons

In the Taskbar image on the previous page, three icons are shown to the right of the Start Button. These icons are added by default and are always present, unless you choose to unpin them, as previously described. The three icons are as follows:

 Clicking this icon launches the Internet Explorer Web browser. (Alternative browsers are discussed later in this book).

 This icon opens Windows Explorer which displays all your libraries of Documents, Music, Pictures, etc., and allows you to browse the hard disc, CDs/DVDs, etc.

 The Windows Media Player is launched by this icon, enabling you to play music and videos and organise your media into various categories and create playlists.

Thumbnails on the Taskbar

If you allow the cursor to hover over a Taskbar icon for a program currently running, one or more small windows or *thumbnails* appear, showing you miniature versions of the screens for that program. For example, hovering over the Internet Explorer icon displays thumbnails of any open Web pages, as shown below. If the thumbnail represents a Web page or a program currently in the background, clicking anywhere on the thumbnail causes the Web page to open up on the screen.

Jump Lists

These provide a very quick way of returning to recently used documents, files and Web pages and then opening them on the screen. To open a Jump List, right-click over the icon for the relevant program on the Taskbar at the bottom of the screen.

Jump Lists and Documents

Shown on the right is the jump list obtained by right-clicking over the

 Microsoft Publisher icon on the Taskbar, shown on the left.

Listed under **Recent** are four documents I have been working on in the last few days. A single click on a document name such as **Getting Online.pub** opens the document, filling the screen. There is also an option to pin the icon for the Publisher program to the Taskbar. **Close window** at the bottom of the Jump List shuts the program down.

If you right-click over a document in the list, there is an option to pin the document permanently to the Jump List. The document **Windows 7 Revealed.pub** has been pinned to the Jump List, as shown in the window above.

Jump Lists and Folders

If you right-click the Windows Explorer icon shown on the right, a Jump List appears containing the names of folders you visit frequently. A single click opens the folder to reveal the files within.

Jump Lists and Web Sites

Shown on the right is the jump list obtained by right-clicking the Internet Explorer icon on the Taskbar, shown on the left.

The **Google** Internet *search engine* shown on the right can be launched from this Jump List with a single click.

Listed under **Frequent** on the right above are the names of Web sites which have been visited recently. A single click opens a Web site. Clicking **Start InPrivate Browsing** shown on the right above stops Internet Explorer from saving information about your personal browsing activities, such as your browsing History and Temporary Internet Files.

Open new tab shown in the screenshot above is used when you want several Web sites open simultaneously; tabs allow you to switch quickly between Web sites, as shown below. Three tabs are shown below at the bottom of an extract from Internet Explorer. These are **Hotmail, News, Sport**, **Homepage for Babani Books** and **AA Route Planner**. Tabs are discussed in more detail later in the chapter on Internet Explorer.

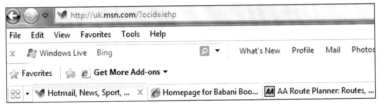

Maximizing, Minimizing and Closing Windows

Windows can be displayed in several different ways:

- Maximized so that they fill the whole screen.

- Minimized so that they only appear as icons on the Windows Taskbar across the bottom of the screen.

- As a thumbnail or miniature preview of the maximized window.

- Displayed at an intermediate size in between the size of the thumbnail and size of the maximized window.

A window which is currently minimized as an icon on the Taskbar can be restored to its original size by clicking the icon. Alternatively allow the cursor to hover over the icon and click the thumbnail which appears, as shown on the right.

A window which is currently open on the screen can be minimized by clicking the icon on the left of the three icons shown on the right. The middle icon either maximizes an intermediate size window or restores a maximized window down to its original size. The icon on the right closes the window and shuts down the program.

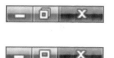

Aero Shake

With several windows open, place the cursor in the top bar of a window you want to concentrate on. Hold down the left-hand button and shake the mouse. All other windows are minimized, leaving the required window displayed on the screen.

Displaying Two Windows Side by Side

It's often useful to have two windows open on the screen at the same time; for example, to make comparisons or to refer to information in one window while writing a report in the other. It's also easier to copy information from one window and "paste" it into the other when they are displayed simultaneously.

To display two windows side by side, place the cursor in the Title Bar across the top of the window. Keeping the left-hand button held down, drag the window to the left-hand edge of the screen until an outline of the window appears, then release the button. Now repeat the process by dragging the other window to the right side of the screen until the window's outline appears.

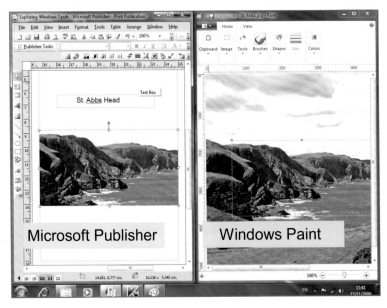

In the example above, part of a photograph displayed in Windows Paint in the right-hand window has been copied onto a page in Microsoft Publisher in the left-hand window. This was done using the **Copy** and **Paste** commands from the Paint and Publisher menus.

The Notification Area of the Taskbar

As discussed earlier, the left-hand side and middle section of the Taskbar are mainly used for launching programs. On the right of the Taskbar is a group of small icons and numbers, known as the Notification Area and shown below.

Viewing the Desktop

You may wish to return to view the Desktop, perhaps to access an icon for a favourite file or program. (An icon for a program can be placed on the Desktop by right-clicking the program in the All Programs menu and selecting **Send to** and then **Desktop** (**Create shortcut**)). Click the small **Show desktop** rectangle on the extreme right of the Taskbar, to display the Desktop and minimize the currently open windows. Click the rectangle again to restore the windows to their previous state. Hovering the cursor over the rectangle gives a temporary view of the Desktop.

Language

EN on the Taskbar above shows that the language has been set to English on this particular computer. Right-click over **EN** to display a menu which allows you to change the language used.

Hidden Icons

To prevent cluttering the Taskbar, certain icons remain hidden. Clicking the small arrow to the right of **EN** on the Taskbar shown below right reveals the hidden icons for various utilities such as an anti-virus program, and a program to manage the printer. Clicking **Customize...** shown on the right allows you to select which icons and notifications are to appear on the Taskbar.

Installing New Hardware

When your computer detects that a new piece of hardware has been attached to it, Windows has to install special software called *drivers*. You are informed of the progress of the installation process in the Notification Area as shown below.

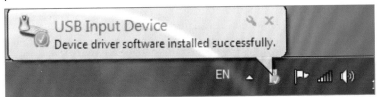

Solve PC issues

Clicking the small flag icon shown above and on the right warns of issues which require attention, such as a recommendation to use **Windows Backup** to make duplicate copies of important files. Or you might be advised to improve security or add anti-virus protection.

The Network Icon

This shows whether the computer is connected to the Internet and/or a local network. Clicking this icon leads to the Windows Network and Sharing Center, giving information about your computers and any networks they are connected to. If the computer is not connected to the Internet, an orange star appears over the network icon on the Taskbar, as shown on the right.

The Speakers Icon

Clicking this icon displays a slider which allows you to adjust the volume of your speakers; right-clicking the icon leads to various menus for setting the sound controls on your computer. These include the sounds emitted by the computer during various Windows operations, such as starting up, for example.

The Control Panel

This is a very important Windows feature, used for making changes to the settings for the hardware and software on the computer. The **Control Panel** opens in its own window, as shown below, after you click its name on the right-hand side of the Start Menu shown on page 58.

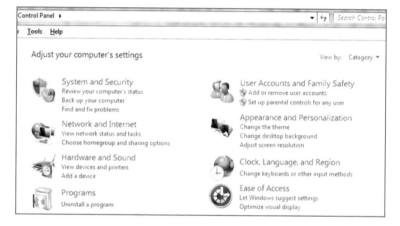

The **Control Panel** shown above is displayed in **Category** view. As can be seen there are categories to manage all aspects of the computer, such as the security settings, changing the appearance of the windows and installing and removing hardware and software. The **Ease of Access Center,** discussed in the next chapter, allows you to set up your computer to provide help with any special needs such as impaired eyesight.

The view of the **Control Panel** can be changed by clicking the small arrow to the right of **View by** shown above. This allows you to switch between **Category** view and **Large icons** and **Small icons**

as shown on the right. When an icons view is selected, all the separate tools in the **Control Panel** are displayed on the screen.

The Computer Window

Clicking the word **Computer** on the Start Menu shown on page 58 opens up a window showing all your disc drives, etc.

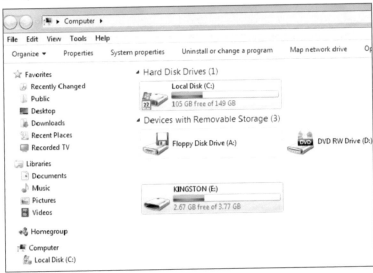

In the **Computer** window above, it can be seen that the hard disc designated **Local Disk (C:)** has 105GB free out of a total of 149GB. **Kingston (E:)** above is a removable *flash drive.* This takes the form of a "dongle", a device which plugs into one of the USB ports (as described on page 15). When you attach a removable device such as a flash drive, external hard disc or digital camera it appears in the Computer window with the next available drive letter. For example, when I plug in my digital camera, it shows up as  **Removable Disk (F:)** in the Computer window.

The left-hand panel of the Computer window above lists all of your folders and libraries containing documents, music and video, etc., as well as any external hard discs and removable drives plugged into the USB ports.

If you double-click the name of a disc drive, etc., such as the **Local Disk (C:)** in the Computer window shown on the previous page, you can display the folders, sub-folders and files as shown on the right.

A folder or file is opened by double-clicking its name or icon, such as the Word file shown on the right. A file opens up in

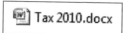

its associated program; for example, a report or letter might open in Microsoft Word. In this example the file **Tax 2010** is saved in the **Tax** sub-folder within the **Accounts** folder on the **(C:)** drive.

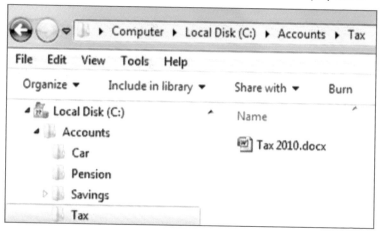

The discs, folders and files on your computer can also be displayed after clicking the Windows Explorer icon shown on the right and on the Taskbar below.

Right-click a file or folder to carry out management tasks such as renaming, copying or deleting a file or folder.

6

Windows 7 Help for Users with Special Needs

Introduction

Windows 7 contains a number of **Ease of Access** features designed to help common impairments such as:

- Poor Eyesight
- Reduced Manual Dexterity
- Impaired Hearing

If you know the special needs help you require, the **Ease of Access** menu can be quickly launched by selecting **Start**, **All Programs**, **Accessories** and **Ease of Access**.

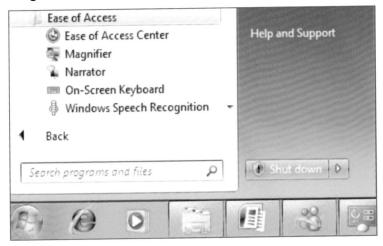

Click the individual tools such as the **Magnifier** or **Narrator** to open them directly. Alternatively click **Ease of Access Center** shown above to investigate any special needs tools you may require, as discussed in more detail on the next page.

The Ease of Access Center

Click **Start**, **Control Panel** and **Ease of Access** as shown on the right. Then select **Ease of Access Center** from the **Ease of Access** window, as shown below.

Ease of Access Center
Let Windows suggest settings   Optimize visual display   Replace sounds with visual cues
Change how your mouse works   Change how your keyboard works

When you click **Ease of Access Center** shown above, all of the special needs tools and help facilities are displayed in the window shown below.

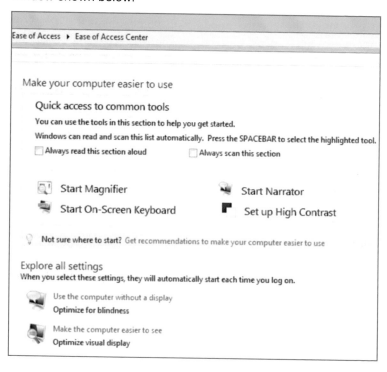

Ease of Access ▸ Ease of Access Center

Make your computer easier to use

Quick access to common tools

You can use the tools in this section to help you get started.

Windows can read and scan this list automatically. Press the SPACEBAR to select the highlighted tool.

☐ Always read this section aloud   ☐ Always scan this section

Start Magnifier   Start Narrator

Start On-Screen Keyboard   Set up High Contrast

Not sure where to start? Get recommendations to make your computer easier to use

Explore all settings

When you select these settings, they will automatically start each time you log on.

Use the computer without a display
Optimize for blindness

Make the computer easier to see
Optimize visual display

The Magnifier

As shown in the previous window, you can go directly to any of the various **Ease of Access** tools, such as the **Magnifier**, for example. The **Magnifier** produces various enlarged views of text and graphics, as discussed shortly.

The Narrator

The **Narrator** reads out aloud the contents of the windows displayed on the screen, including titles, menu options, features such as buttons and check boxes, and keys as they are typed.

The On-screen Keyboard

If you find a normal keyboard difficult to use, you can "type" by using the mouse to click the letters on a virtual keyboard displayed on the screen.

High Contrast

This option makes the screen easier to read by increasing the contrast on colours. **High Contrast** is switched on and off by simultaneously pressing down **Alt** + left **Shift** + **PRINT SCREEN** (may be marked **Prt Sc** on your keyboard).

The above features are discussed in more detail shortly.

Finding Out Your Own Special Needs

If you are not sure which tools you need to help you, the **Ease of Access Center** allows you to select your particular needs from several lists of impairments. Then a list of recommended settings is produced which you may choose to switch on, if you wish. To start entering any difficulties you may have, click on **Get recommendations to make your computer easier to use**, highlighted in yellow in the **Ease of Access Center** window, as shown below and on the previous page.

Not sure where to start? Get recommendations to make your computer easier to use

You are presented with a series of statements under the headings **Eyesight**, **Dexterity**, **Hearing**, **Speech** and **Reasoning**. Each statement is preceded by a check box, which you can tick by clicking with the mouse if it applies to you. For example, the **Eyesight** statements are shown below:

Eyesight (1 of 5)

Select all statements that apply to you:

☑ Images and text on TV are difficult to see (even when I'm wearing glasses).

☐ Lighting conditions make it difficult to see images on my monitor.

☐ I am blind.

☐ I have another type of vision impairment (even if glasses correct it).

After you click **Next**, the investigation of your needs continues with the statements on **Dexterity**, **Hearing**, **Speech** and **Reasoning**. Finally you are presented with a list of recommended settings which you may choose to switch on by clicking to tick the check box, as shown below:

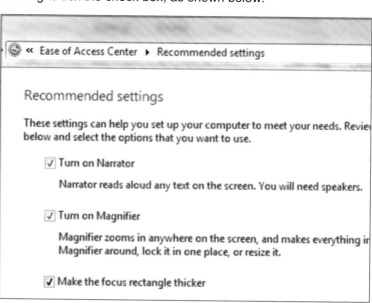

« Ease of Access Center ▸ Recommended settings

Recommended settings

These settings can help you set up your computer to meet your needs. Revie below and select the options that you want to use.

☑ Turn on Narrator

Narrator reads aloud any text on the screen. You will need speakers.

☑ Turn on Magnifier

Magnifier zooms in anywhere on the screen, and makes everything ir Magnifier around, lock it in one place, or resize it.

☑ Make the focus rectangle thicker

The list of **Recommended settings** shown previously may also include options to change the colour and size of the mouse pointers as shown below:

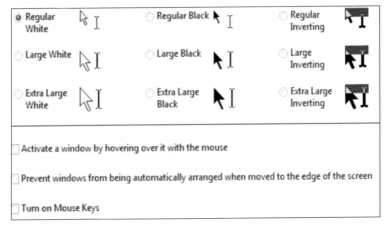

The other options include **Turn on Sticky Keys**. Some keyboard "shortcuts" normally require three keys on the keyboard to be pressed simultaneously. **Sticky Keys** allow these operations to be reduced to a single key press.

Turn on Mouse Keys shown above enables the numeric keypad (on the right of the keyboard) and also the arrow keys, to move the mouse pointer around the screen.

When you've finished selecting your **Ease of Access** recommended settings, click **Apply** and **Save** near the bottom of the screen. From now on, each time you start the computer, your chosen features, such as the **Magnifier** or the **On-Screen Keyboard**, will start up automatically.

At the bottom of the list of **Ease of Access** recommendations is a clickable link to a Web site giving further information about organisations and products (known as *assistive technologies*) intended to make computers easier to use.

Learn about additional assistive technologies online

Enlarging the Display with the Magnifier

Click **Start Magnifier** as shown on page 72. The small **Magnifier** window opens, as shown on the right. Click the + or – signs to increase or decrease the size of the text on the screen. Click the small arrow on the right of **Views** above and you can choose whether to enlarge the **Full screen** or just a small movable rectangular area around the cursor, known as the **Lens,** as shown below.

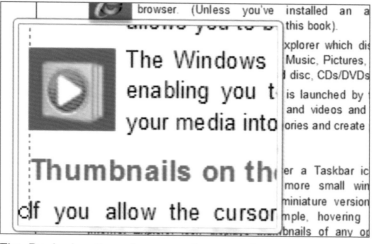

The **Docked** option allows you to move the cursor around a normal sized screen window while displaying, in a separate window, an enlargement of the screen around the cursor position. If the **Magnifier** is running but has not been used for a while, it changes to an icon for a magnifying glass. Click this icon to display the **Magnifier** window again, as shown at the top of this page.

Using the Narrator

The **Narrator** reads out aloud the details of any windows you've opened, toolbars, menu options, the keys you've pressed and any text in documents on the screen. The **Narrator** is launched by clicking **Start Narrator** in the **Ease of Access Center**, as shown on page 72. After a few seconds the **Narrator** window appears, as shown below, allowing you to make various adjustments to the settings. When the **Narrator** is running, an icon is displayed on the Windows 7 Taskbar, as shown on the right.

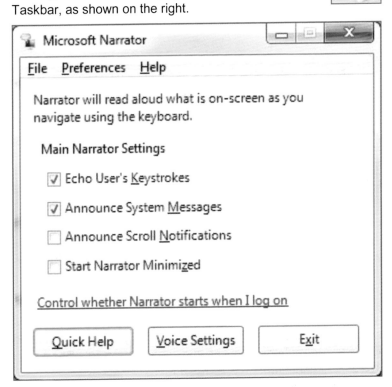

Press **Exit** to stop using the **Narrator**. More details about the **Narrator** can be found after clicking the Start Button, then **Help and Support** and entering **Narrator** in the Search Bar.

The On-screen Keyboard

If you have trouble using an ordinary keyboard, you may find it easier to use the virtual keyboard provided in Windows 7. From the **Ease of Access Center** shown on page 72, select **Start On-Screen Keyboard**. An image of a keyboard appears on the screen as shown below. There is also an icon for the **On-Screen Keyboard** on the Windows 7 Taskbar, as shown on the right.

The **On-Screen Keyboard** is operated by a mouse or other device, such as a joystick. Place the cursor where you want to begin typing and point to and click the required letters.

Upper case (i.e. capital) letters are obtained after clicking one of the on-screen **Shift** keys shown above. The **On-Screen Keyboard** can be moved to a convenient position by dragging in the area to the right of the words **On-Screen Keyboard**.

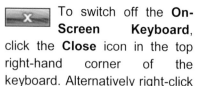 To switch off the **On-Screen Keyboard**, click the **Close** icon in the top right-hand corner of the keyboard. Alternatively right-click  the Taskbar icon and click **Close window** on the menu which pops up as shown above. To use the **On-Screen Keyboard** regularly, click **Pin this program to taskbar**.

High Contrast

This option is intended to make the screen easier to read by increasing the contrast on colours. **High Contrast** is switched on and off by simultaneously pressing down **Alt** + left **Shift** + **PRINT SCREEN** (may be marked **Prt Sc** or similar on your keyboard).

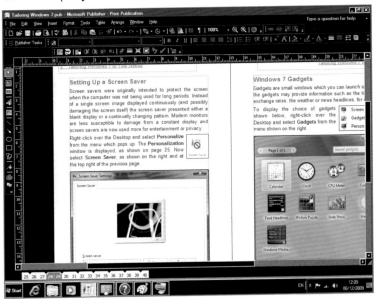

There are several different **High Contrast** themes listed in the **Personalization** section of the **Control Panel**. Right-click over the Windows 7 Desktop and select **Personalize** from the menu which appears. Then scroll down and select one of the **Basic and High Contrast Themes** by clicking, as shown in the extract below.

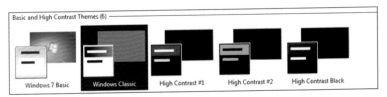

Further Help

There are many companies and organisations offering more specialist help than is provided by the tools available within Windows 7, just discussed. For example, alternative input devices are available for sufferers of illnesses such as Parkinson's Disease or Cerebral Palsy. As mentioned earlier, there is a link, shown below, at the end of the **Ease of Access Recommended settings** in Windows 7.

Learn about additional assistive technologies online

Clicking this link enables you to access a wide range of information on assistive or accessibility issues. There are also links to the Web sites of companies providing specialist devices, for example, the **Head Mounted Mousing Alternative** link below.

Tracker 2000 - Head Mounted Mousing Alternative by Madentec Limited
"Great for Those with Limited Mobility" **More**

You can also carry out your own Internet search for help by entering relevant keywords, such as **disability computer technology** or **special needs computer equipment** or **computer accessibility** into a search engine such as Google.

Click on any of the links (which appear underlined in the list of search results) to view the relevant Web site.

7

Installing and Using Software

Introduction

Microsoft Office 2010 is a suite of several programs based around the word processor Microsoft Word and the spreadsheet Microsoft Excel. These form a major part of the world's leading office software and are discussed shortly; while they are powerful enough for sophisticated business users they are also very user-friendly and suitable for the most inexperienced home user. Microsoft Word can be used for anything from a simple document to a 300-page book including text and pictures. In fact I have used Word to produce nearly 30 books, including many of the "Babani Older Generation" series.

There are several editions of Microsoft Office, but most home and small business users should find Office Home and Student 2010 edition meets most of their needs. There is also a Starter edition which will be provided free with many new computers. This edition includes limited versions of Word and Excel and also some advertising; the Starter edition is intended to allow users to sample Office 2010 before buying one of the full editions.

The programs included with Office 2010 Home and Student edition are Word, Excel, OneNote and PowerPoint. This chapter concentrates on Word and Excel, two of the world's most widely used programs. Access, Outlook and Publisher shown on the right are only limited *trial* versions included with Office 2010 Home and Student edition — you must buy the full versions separately.

Installing Microsoft Office 2010

The Product Key

On the back of an inner plastic case in the Office package is the PRODUCT KEY label. The product key is your licence to install the software – it's used to validate and activate the software so that it can be used on your computer. It's worth making a copy of the 25-character product key and storing it in a safe place. You might have a technical problem later and need to re-install the Office software – virtually impossible without the product key.

During the installation process you will be asked to enter your 25-character product key. If you don't enter a product key you will only be able to fully use the software for 30 days.

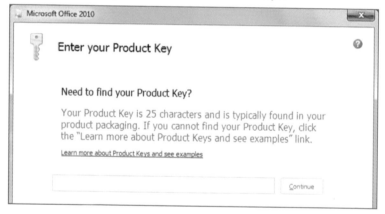

If the product key is genuine, you then click **Continue** to carry on with the installation. After choosing to either **Upgrade** or **Customize** you are presented with a window showing the **Progress** of the installation as a percentage. The installation may appear to do nothing for several minutes. Finally you are informed that the software has been successfully installed. As with many software installations, you need to restart the computer before using the software for the first time.

Activation

Each copy of Microsoft Office has to be *activated* to allow unlimited use on a particular computer. (Office Home & Student 2010 is licensed for up to 3 installations). You are given the choice to activate over the Internet or by telephone. Internet activation occurs automatically; telephone activation requires an assurance that you are not installing too many copies of the software. If you don't activate your copy of Office 2010 you will only be able to use the software for a limited number of sessions.

Launching the Programs

At the end of the installation process you will find entries for **Microsoft Office**, including **Word** and **Excel**, in the **All Programs** menu accessed via the **Start** button in the bottom left-hand corner of the screen, as shown below.

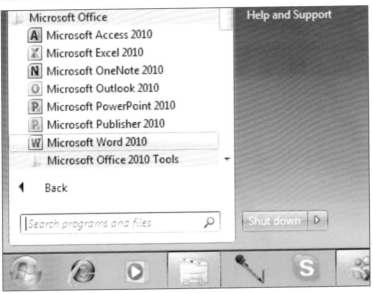

A component program such as Word 2010 is launched by clicking its entry in the **All Programs** menu shown above.

The Tabbed Ribbon

In Office 2010 the traditional drop-down menus such as **File**, **Edit** and **View**, etc., have been replaced by a *tabbed ribbon* as shown below. Ribbons are used in Word, Excel and PowerPoint.

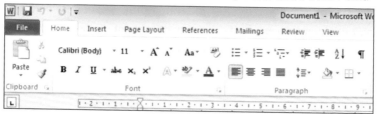

All of the usual tools are still available – it's just that they are presented in a different layout. There is a new **File** tab with options, for example, to **Open**, **Save** and **Print** a document, as shown on the next page. There are various other tabs on the ribbon such as **Home**, **Insert** and **Page Layout**, as shown above. Icons for related tasks are grouped together, such as the **Font** group for changing the style and size of letters. The text formatting tools such as indentation, centring, justification and line spacing are displayed in the **Paragraph** group shown above.

One of the most striking features of the ribbon is that as you change to a different task, the tools on the ribbon change automatically. For example, if you select a picture or image so that it's highlighted in a Word document, the **Picture Tools Format** tab appears, as shown below. Clicking this tab displays a complete set of tools for formatting a picture. An extract from the ribbon with the **Picture Tools Format** tab selected is shown below.

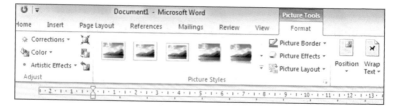

The File Tab in Word 2010 and Excel 2010

When you click the **File** tab shown below, a menu appears with options to carry out major tasks such as saving and printing a document. As shown below, when you click **New**, a choice of templates is presented, providing ready-made formats, artwork and designs appropriate to the new document you wish to create.

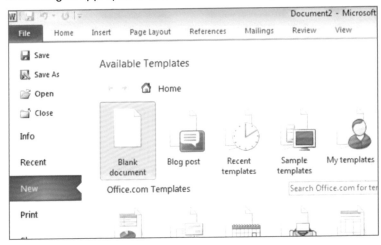

Save and **Save As** shown above are used to make a permanent copy of your work, such as a letter to your car's insurers. This might be saved with a name such as **Accident** and stored as a file in a folder named **Car**, as shown on the next page. By clicking in the left-hand panel in the **Save As** window shown on the next page you can select a folder on your hard disc, in which to save the document. The hard disc is normally called the **(C:)** drive. Alternatively you can select a different storage device such as a plug-in *flash drive* or a *removable hard disc*, (if available}.

When you've used **Save As** to name and save a file in a specific location, later versions of the file can be saved simply by clicking **Save** on the File tab. This overwrites an earlier version of a file with the latest edition. To keep the earlier editions of a file, use a different name each time you save the file.

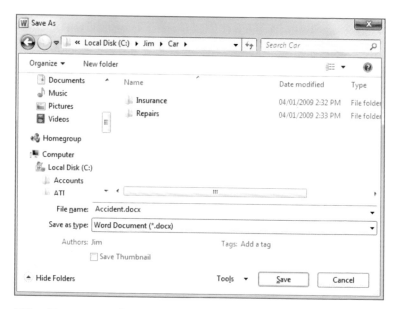

File Formats for Saving Word Documents

The **Save As** option in Word 2010 can be used to save documents in a number of different file formats, as shown below.

Word Document (.docx)

This is the latest format for Word files. To read **.docx** files in earlier versions of Word, download the Office Compatibility Pack from Microsoft Office Online.

Word 97-2003 Document (.doc)

Save in this format if you want to create documents to be read in earlier versions of Word. Word 2010 can open documents created in earlier versions of Word.

PDF (Portable Document Format)

This is a file format which can be read on any type of computer, using a program called Adobe Reader, available as a free download from the Adobe Web site at **www.adobe.co.uk**. XPS is a similar format provided by Microsoft.

Introducing Word 2010

Word processing is one of the most frequently used applications of computers and Microsoft Word is the undisputed world leader. The modern word processor is capable of creating all sorts of documents, such as:

- Letters to friends and relatives

- Reports including tables and graphs

- A club newsletter or a parish magazine

- Leaflets and flyers including artwork and pictures, with text in various shapes, known as WordArt, as shown below.

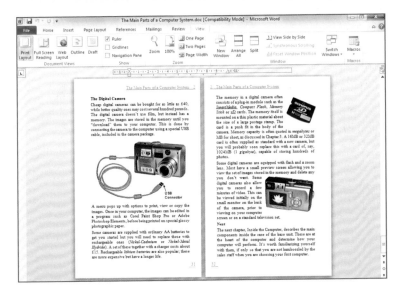

- A novel or book (like this one), as shown in the two-page spread below taken from one of our other books.

Advantages of Word Processors

Word processors are far more versatile than the traditional typewriter; they are easy to use and allow anyone to produce professional-looking documents. Some of the advantages of the word processor are as follows:

- Corrections can be made on the screen before printing on paper, so there is no evidence of any alterations. Several copies can easily be printed.

- Documents are saved on disc and can be retrieved later. This allows a document to be used again, perhaps with small changes such as a new date. There is no need to retype the whole document.

- Text can be *edited* more easily – whole blocks of text can be inserted, deleted or moved to a new position in the document.

- The *Find and Replace* feature enables a word (or group of words) to be exchanged for another word (or words), wherever they occur in a document.

- Text can be formatted with effects such as bold and italic and in various fonts or styles of lettering, such as the Algerian font shown below.

ALGERIAN

- The layout of the page can easily be changed or with text set in tables or newspaper-style columns.

- Modern word processors contain many additional features such as spelling and grammar checkers, a thesaurus and a word count facility.

Introducing Excel 2010

Excel is the world's leading spreadsheet program; it is designed to work on tables of figures, reducing long and complex calculations to simple point-and-click operations using a mouse. Excel 2010 is operated using a new ribbon interface, similar to the one used in Word 2010, as described earlier in this chapter.

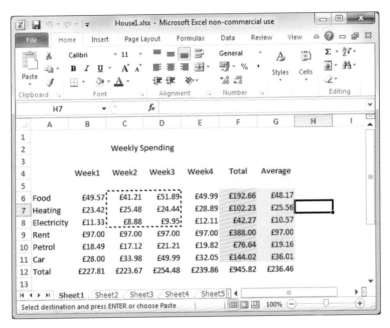

Although Excel is mainly used for calculations, it can also be used as a type of database for keeping text-based records and sorting them into order. I have used Excel for storing hundreds of names and addresses; these are then input into the mail merge facility in Microsoft Word for the automatic printing of address labels, saving a huge amount of time.

Recalculation

The spreadsheet allows you to speculate on the effect of possible changes, such as an increase in the price of petrol. These changes can be fed into the spreadsheet, which automatically recalculates all of the totals, etc., affected by the change. The *recalculation* feature is one of the main advantages of spreadsheet programs and can save many hours of work compared with traditional methods of calculation using pencil and paper or electronic calculators.

Graphs and Charts

Apart from the ability to perform the whole range of mathematical calculations, data can be presented in the form of pie charts, bar charts and line graphs, etc.

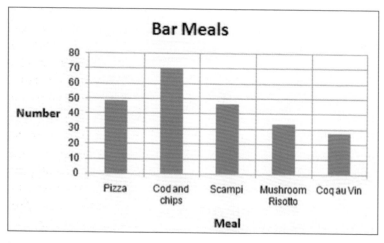

Both the spreadsheet itself and the charts produced from it can be imported into documents in a word processor. This feature is useful, for example, when producing a report on sales performance in a business.

Spreadsheets are discussed in more detail in our book "An Introduction to Excel Spreadsheets", reference BP 701, from Bernard Babani (publishing) Ltd.

8

Good Housekeeping

Introduction

Modern computers are very reliable if treated with care; for a good many years I've had three or more budget computers up and running at home and there have been no major problems. However, there are steps you can take to keep your computer running reliably and also safe from external threats. Normal running of your computer creates a lot of debris in the form of redundant and disorganized files and so your hard disc can benefit from a bit of care and attention from time to time.

Unfortunately computer crime is on the increase and there are plenty of highly skilled hackers using the Internet who may try to get hold of your personal information, such as bank account details. In addition there is the constant threat of viruses or malicious software (*malware*), spread to your computer from the Internet and e-mails. Malware is software which may cause damage to your computer's files or theft of your data and inconvenience to yourself.

You might let children or grandchildren "play" on your computer or "improve" it by changing a few settings or installing some software of their own. While most children are sensible and many are brilliant computer whiz-kids, as a former teacher I know there are some children who can wreak havoc, either accidentally or deliberately. If you're using a computer for serious work, whether business, social or charitable, it's a good idea if that machine is kept separate from any computer used by other people for entertainment.

This chapter describes some simple steps you can take to keep your computer running at its best level of performance; they don't require any special skill, won't cost a lot of money and most will only take a few minutes.

Disk Cleanup

During normal running, your computer creates a lot of temporary files on the hard disc. When you browse the Internet, the content of Web pages is temporarily saved so the site can be viewed more quickly next time. When using a program like Word 2010, more temporary files are created. These take up disc space and if ignored for a long time may cause the computer to run slowly.

To remove these redundant files cluttering up your hard disc, run **Disk Cleanup**, once a week say, by selecting **Start**, **All Programs**, **Accessories**, **System Tools** and **Disk Cleanup**.

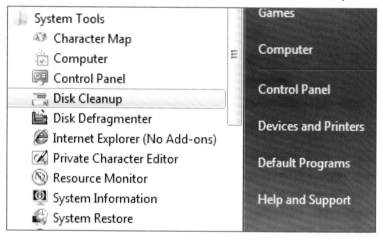

After you've used **Disk Cleanup** once, in future the program can be launched straightaway from the main **Start** menu. A window opens giving you the chance to clean up just your own files or the files of all users of the computer. After making a selection, you choose the drive you wish to clean up – usually drive **(C:)**. **Disk Cleanup** then takes a few minutes to calculate how much disc space can be saved by deleting unnecessary files.

After calculating the potential gain in recovered disc space, the unnecessary files are listed, as shown below.

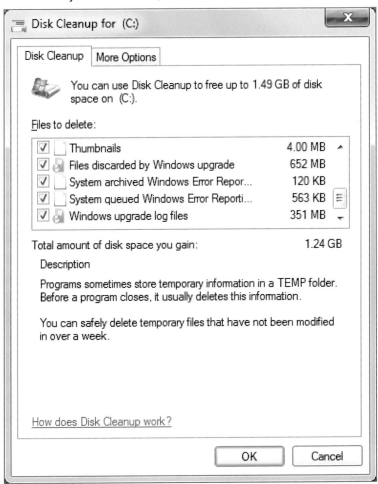

When you click on an entry, such as **Temporary Internet Files**, the purpose of the files is explained in the **Description** panel as well as guidance on the effects of removing them.

Decide which files are to be deleted and click their check boxes so that a tick appears. The amount of free disc space which can be gained is displayed in the window shown on the previous page. Click **OK** and a small window appears asking if you are sure you want to delete the files. Then click the **Delete Files** button to complete the cleanup operation.

If you click the **More Options** tab shown on the previous page and below, this provides an option to free up more disc space by deleting programs which you no longer use. Click the **Clean up...** button shown below to select the programs to be deleted.

A further option allows you to delete early copies of restore points which are no longer needed. Restore points are "snapshots" of critical settings which can be used to return a faulty computer to a previous, healthy configuration.

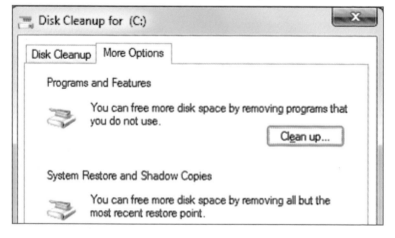

You can check the free space on your hard disc by clicking the **Start** orb, then click **Computer** off the **Start** menu. Click on the hard disc, typically labelled as Local Disk (C:) to highlight it and display the remaining free space, e.g. **105GB free of 149GB** as shown on the right.

Using Disk Defragmenter

After you've been using your computer for a while, many files will have been repeatedly modified and resaved. The original files and the changes may become separated, scattered about the hard disc in different places. This will impair the performance of the computer when it tries to open a file which is spread around many different locations; _defragmentation_ is a process which rearranges the files on the hard disc to make the computer run more efficiently. In Windows 7, the **Disk Defragmenter** program is scheduled to run automatically. Alternatively it can be launched by clicking the **Start** orb then selecting **All Programs**, **Accessories**, **System Tools** and **Disk Defragmenter**.

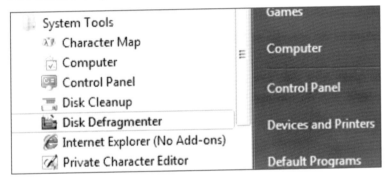

After you've used **Disk Defragmenter** the first time, the program can be launched in future by clicking its name, which by now will be listed on the **Start** menu.

The **Disk Defragmenter** window opens, as shown on the next page. In this particular example, the **Disk Defragmenter** program has been scheduled to run once a week, but you can change this if you wish after clicking **Configure schedule....**

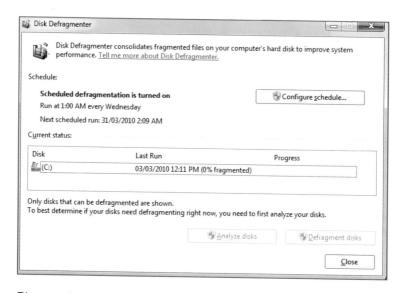

Please also note in the **Disk Defragmenter** window above, the **Defragment disks** button allows you to manually start an immediate defragmentation whenever you think it might be beneficial. Select the drive you wish to defragment, usually **(C:)** then click the **Defragment disks** button. The **Analyze disks** button allows you to find out the extent to which a disc is defragmented. The defragmentation process may take several minutes or a few hours, depending on the size and state of the hard disc. Fortunately you can continue to use the computer while the **Disk Defragmenter** program is running.

Regular Servicing

It's recommended that, in order to keep your computer running efficiently, **Disk Cleanup** and **Disk Defragmenter** are run regularly – at least once a week, especially if the computer is heavily used. If the computer appears to be running slowly for no obvious reason, it may be worth carrying out an immediate defragmentation.

Checking Your Computer's Security

Windows 7 provides a battery of security features designed to prevent criminal and malicious access to your computer. You can easily carry out an audit of the security settings on your computer. Click the Start Button and then select **Control Panel** from the right-hand panel of the Start Menu. After the **Control Panel** opens, select **Review your computer's status**, as shown on the right. Click **Security** and then the **Action Center**, shown below, displays a list of the various security features and their status.

System and Security
Review your computer's status
Back up your computer
Find and fix problems

System and Security ▸ Action Center

Review recent messages and resolve problems
Action Center has detected one or more issues for you to review.

Security

Network firewall   On
    Norton Internet Security reports that it is currently turned on.
    View installed firewall programs

Windows Update   On
    Windows will automatically install updates as they become available.

Virus protection   On
    Norton Internet Security reports that it is up to date and virus scanning is on.

Spyware and unwanted software protection   On
    Windows Defender and Norton Internet Security both report that they are turned on
    Note: Running two or more antispyware programs at the same time can cause your

The Windows 7 Firewall

This is a piece of software designed to prevent hackers from invading your computer via the Internet. Suspicious information is blocked from entering (or leaving) your computer. If you install an Internet security package such as Norton, Kaspersky, F-Secure or McAfee, these will provide a firewall that you can switch on. Some wireless routers also include a built-in hardware firewall.

Window 7 also includes its own software firewall; this should be switched on if you do not have a firewall provided by a third party Internet security program. From the **Control Panel**, select **System and Security** and then **Windows Firewall**. Then click **Turn Windows Firewall on or off**, as shown on the right.

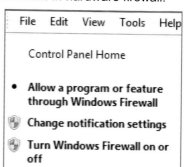

The **Customize Settings** window opens, as shown below. This allows you to turn the Windows Firewall on or off.

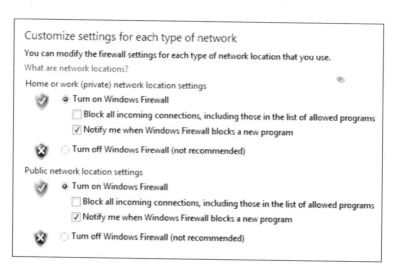

Windows Update

Operating systems such as Windows 7 are under constant development; Microsoft regularly distributes software modifications and "fixes" to overcome problems which have arisen during the use of Windows. These software modifications often involve improvements to Windows security and they are delivered to your computer over the Internet. Windows Update should be permanently switched on after clicking the Start Button and selecting **All Programs** and **Windows Update**.

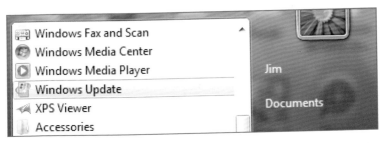

As shown below, you are informed when updates are available. These are classified as either **important** or **optional**; after clicking the appropriate links shown in blue you can review the updates and install them if you wish, by clicking the **Install updates** button.

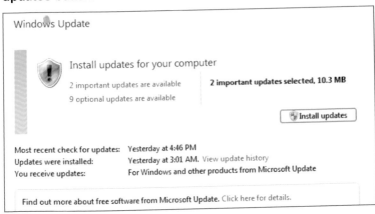

Malware Protection

Malware is an abbreviation for malicious software and refers to computer viruses and other malevolent programs; the computer virus is a small program written for the purpose of causing damage and inconvenience. In the worst case it might cause the entire contents of a hard disc to be wiped.

It's essential that you have an anti-virus program installed and this should have a database which is regularly updated with the latest virus definitions. Then the program can detect and destroy the latest viruses as well as many thousands of older ones.

Well known providers of anti-virus software include Kaspersky, Norton (Symantec) and F-Secure. Many companies also produce complete Internet security packages which include anti-virus software as well as firewalls and protection against spyware – software designed to collect personal information from someone else's computer.

Anti-virus/Internet security packages typically cost £20 – £50 and this usually includes the software on CD or DVD and a year's updates of virus definitions. Updates are normally downloaded automatically from the Internet. Some companies now allow one software package to be legally installed on up to three computers. Subscriptions to an anti-virus package are normally renewed annually.

As discussed earlier, you can check that your anti-virus protection is on after clicking the Start Button and selecting **Control Panel**, **Review your computer's status** (under **System and Security**) then clicking **Security**. The example below shows that this particular computer has virus protection enabled.

Virus protection	On
Kaspersky Internet Security reports that it is up to date and virus scanning is on.	

The Anatomy of a Computer

Introduction

This chapter has been left until last because it explains the technical terms, jargon, etc., which many people find off-putting — terms like "RAM", "megabytes", "motherboard" and "dual-core" processor for example. However, it is hoped that the following pages will provide a clear understanding of the functions of the main components common to all computers and serve as a reference section to explain the unavoidable jargon in the rest of the book.

In recent years computers have become much easier to use and are now a popular consumer product, a versatile tool to which many people have access; it's no longer essential to be a technical expert to use a laptop or desktop computer. Many people now surf the Internet, send an e-mail or type a report, without any idea of what's happening under the casing of their machine; in much the same way you can drive a car without knowing what's under the bonnet. However, although you may be able to use your computer quite happily, without some understanding of its vital innards you probably won't make the most of your computing activities.

Of course, behind many technically-unaware computer users there is often a computer guru in the background, to be called upon whenever necessary to solve problems or give advice. Perhaps your son, daughter, whiz-kid grandchild or a helpful neighbour acts as your computing lifeline. This is fine unless the computing guru moves away or is no longer available for any reason.

If you depend on someone else to solve your computing problems, think how much better it would be to become more independent and self-reliant. At the same time you would gain self-esteem and, perhaps, respect amongst your friends and family by increasing your own technical prowess.

It's not difficult to understand the basic operation of a computer, provided any jargon is clearly explained in simple language. The next few pages describe the most important components which are present in every computer; these notes are intended to provide a basic knowledge of each component and its function. This should give you a better understanding of your computer and in particular should help you to:

- Make informed choices when buying new equipment.

- Avoid being blinded with science when dealing with "smart alec" sales people.

- Hold your own when talking to computer-literate friends and "geeks" in social situations.

- Astound your children and grandchildren with your new-found expertise.

- Improve your computer's performance by knowing which are the critical components to upgrade.

- Understand technical problems and attempt solutions.

- Save money and avoid being ripped off by unscrupulous computer repairers.

- Gain confidence to join a local computer class.

The next few pages show how you can discover the specification of your own computer and goes on to explain the functions of the key components which are essential to all computers.

Checking the Specification of Your Computer

Click the **Start** button at the bottom left-hand corner of the screen and then click **Control Panel** from the right of the **Start Menu**. The **Control Panel** window opens, displaying a large number of categories. Click **System and Security** and from the window which opens, select **System**, as shown below.

System and Security
Review your computer's status
Back up your computer
Find and fix problems

System
View amount of RAM and processor speed   Check the Windows Experience Index
Allow remote access   See the name of this computer   Device Manager

The **System** window opens, as shown below; this gives, amongst other things, the amount of memory (RAM) and the type and the make, model and speed of the processor. These components are discussed in more detail in the rest of this chapter. **The Windows Experience Index** is a measure of the computer's overall performance in the range of 1.0 to 7.9. A computer with an index of 2.0 can run general office software, while a figure of 3.0 is required to run the more demanding 3D Aero graphics in Windows 7.

View basic information about your computer

Windows edition

Windows 7 Home Premium

Copyright © 2009 Microsoft Corporation. All rights reserved.

Get more features with a new edition of Windows 7

System

Rating: **3.4** Windows Experience Index

Processor: AMD Athlon(tm) Processor LE-1640   2.60 GHz

Installed memory (RAM):   2.00 GB (1.87 GB usable)

System type: 32-bit Operating System

The Processor

This is also known as the CPU or Central Processing Unit. The processor is the "brains" of any computer; the processor itself is an unimpressive-looking flat chip, as shown on the right. Several hundred small pins are used to connect the processor to the motherboard, the large circuit board (page 115) into which all the other components are connected.

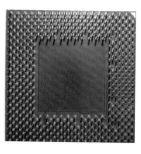

An AMD Athlon processor

The processor executes the programs, i.e. sets of instructions, which tell the computer what to do. A program is temporarily loaded into the computer's memory from the hard disc. (Memory and hard discs are discussed shortly).

Data in a computer is represented in the *binary code* as strings of 0s and 1s (*bits*). The data travels between components inside the computer,

The processor socket on the motherboard

such as the memory and the processor, along parallel wires on the motherboard (page 115). These parallel wires are known as the *data highway* or the *data bus,* typically 32 bits or 64 bits wide, for example. The greater the width of the data bus, the faster the computer's performance.

A very simple example of a program would be to fetch, from the memory, two numbers which you had typed in. Then add them together in the processor and transfer the answer to a section of memory used for the screen display.

The processor is the powerhouse of the computer and generates a lot of heat. This heat is dissipated using a metal *heat sink* and a *cooling fan* as shown on the right. These sit on top of the processor. Laptop computers, being much smaller than desktop machines, are designed to run slower so that they generate less heat in their confined space. In addition, laptops also have a small heat sink, fan and pipes designed to dissipate the heat generated by the processor.

Heat sink and fan

Processor Speed in Gigahertz

The processor incorporates a *clock* which generates electronic pulses or cycles. This determines the speed the computer can carry out instructions and move data around.

The speed of the processor is crucial to the way the computer performs; the example at the bottom of page 103 shows that the processor has a speed of 2.60GHz (or Gigahertz). 1GHz is a measure of frequency and means 1,000,000,000 cycles per second.

I often use a 1.60GHz Windows 7 computer for general tasks such as typesetting books like this one, creating spreadsheets (financial calculations) and surfing the Internet. The performance of a 1.60GHz processor is quite adequate for this type of work. However, for certain applications, such as complex graphics, multimedia work and the latest games, a more powerful processor may be required. Processor speeds ranging from 1 to 3GHz are typical on new computers at the time of writing.

Speeding Up the Computer

It may be possible to improve the performance of a computer by fitting a faster processor, which must be compatible with the motherboard. The old processor is removed after raising a small lever and the new processor is simply plugged in.

You can speed up a processor by "over-clocking", i.e. increasing the processor clock speed; however, this is not recommended as it may result in overheating and invalidation of the computer's warranty.

The CPU Cache

Many advertisements refer to a computer having a *1MB cache* or perhaps a *4MB or 8MB cache* on a more expensive machine. The CPU cache is extra memory within the CPU itself, used to speed up the computer. Frequently used data is temporarily stored in the cache since this is quicker than fetching it repeatedly from the main memory, which is further away across the motherboard. (Memory and megabytes (MB) are discussed shortly).

Multi-Core Processors

Some of the latest CPUs have two processor *cores* mounted on a single chip, examples being the Intel Core 2 Duo and the AMD Athlon X2. These *dual core processors* are faster because they are capable of *multi-tasking* (running two or more programs simultaneously). *Triple* and *Quad core* processors are also available, especially for demanding applications requiring great computing power, such as some games, graphics and multi-media work.

Well-known modern processors are the Athlon, Sempron and Turion from AMD (Advanced Micro Devices, Inc) and the Celeron, Pentium and Core 2 Duo made by the Intel Corporation.

Ordinary single core processors can be bought for as little as £30 or less, while the latest multi-core devices may cost several hundred pounds.

The Memory or RAM

One definition of a computer is a machine which can carry out a sequence of stored instructions; these instructions are known as a *program* and they are stored in the computer's memory or RAM (Random Access Memory). The memory can be thought of as millions of small boxes containing data and instructions. The processor moves data in and out of the memory to carry out a particular task. Any data you type in at the keyboard is stored in the memory.

The memory contains:

- The program or software you are currently using, such as an Internet browser, a game or an e-mail program.

- The data for the current program, such as a file of names and addresses, music or the text of a document.

- The computer's operating system, such as Windows 7, a set of programs responsible for overall control of the computer.

It's important to realise the difference between the RAM, sometimes called the *main memory* , and other forms of storage. The programs and data in the RAM are *temporary*; when you switch the computer off at the end of a session the RAM is emptied. If you've just spent two hours on the computer typing a report or designing a kitchen, for example, the work will be lost unless you record it on some form of *permanent storage*. The latter usually means the computer's internal hard disc or one of the very popular *flash drives* discussed later. Confusion can arise because these forms of permanent storage are also sometimes referred to as memory. Temporary memory in the form of RAM is often defined as *volatile,* while *permanent storage* on magnetic media such as hard discs is *non-volatile* memory.

Memory Modules

Memory or RAM is supplied on modules consisting of a set of chips on a small printed circuit board, as shown below. These are known as *DIMMs* or *Dual In-line Memory Modules*.

A memory module or DIMM

Bits and Bytes — Units of Memory Size

Inside the computer, data and instructions are converted to the *binary code*, where everything is represented by strings of 0s and 1s. So, for example, the letter **A** might be coded as 1000001. The 0s and 1s are known as *binary digits* or *bits* for short. Every letter of the alphabet, number, punctuation mark, keyboard character or program instruction can be represented by groups of bits. These are usually arranged in groups of 8 bits known as a *byte*. As computers have become more powerful over the years, memory sizes have been quoted first in *kilobytes*, then in *megabytes* and nowadays in *gigabytes,* as defined below.

Byte	A group of 8 binary digits (0s and 1s) or bits. A byte may be used to represent a digit 0-9, a letter, punctuation mark or keyboard character, for example.
Kilobyte (K):	1024 bytes
Megabyte (MB):	About 1 million bytes (1,048,576 to be exact).
Gigabyte (GB):	About 1 billion bytes (1,073,741,824 to be exact).

Memory Needed for Windows 7

The computer specification listed at the bottom of page 103 stated a memory (or RAM) size of 2.0GB. Microsoft recommends a minimum RAM of at least 1GB, (preferably 2GB), to get the best from Windows 7. Most new computers are now delivered with a RAM of at least 1GB with higher performance machines having 2 or 4GB or more. The current high performance memory is known as *DDR2 SDRAM* or *double-data-rate two synchronous dynamic random access memory.* Even faster DDR3 RAM is becoming available at the time of writing.

Adding Extra Memory

Increasing the amount of memory can greatly improve a computer's performance and it's a task which anyone can accomplish. We recently added extra memory to a laptop which was running slowly. After a few minutes work to fit extra memory costing £25, the speed of the laptop was dramatically increased.

Before buying new memory always check that it's compatible with your particular motherboard. If necessary take a sample of your existing memory to the supplier. You may be able to increase the memory by adding an extra memory module in an empty slot on the motherboard or by replacing a module with one of higher capacity.

Before starting work, discharge any static electricity, e.g. by touching a water pipe or by using an anti-static wrist strap. Care should be taken to avoid touching the contacts at the bottom of the DIMM. The DIMM is plugged into a slot in the motherboard and held in place by plastic clips at each end, as shown on page 115. A notch on the bottom of the module engages with a spigot on the motherboard, preventing you from fitting it the wrong way round. If the memory is faulty or incorrectly fitted, the computer will "beep" on starting up. Prices of memory fluctuate but currently 1GB of DDR2 memory is about £25 and a 2GB module costs around £45.

Checking Your Hard Disc Capacity

Click the **Start** button at the bottom left of the screen to open the **Start Menu**. Now click **Computer** on the **Start Menu** and a window opens, revealing all of the disc resources on your computer, as shown in the extract below.

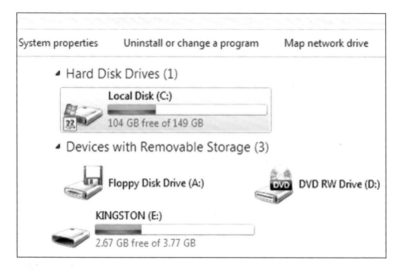

As shown above, the hard disc drive on this particular computer has a total capacity of 149GB. Being a fairly new machine, there is still 104GB free. (Gigabytes (GB) are defined on page 108). The hard disc drive is also known as the hard *disk* drive using American spelling, or more simply the hard drive, the **(C:)** drive or **(D:)** drive if two hard drives are fitted to the computer.

A 149GB in the example above hard disc would, for example, have the capacity to store over 100,000 photographs, 40,000 music tracks or more than 200 videos. A photo copied straight from a digital camera can easily take up 500KB — 1MB or more on the hard disc. This chapter, including all the text and images takes up 5.79MB as a file in Microsoft Publisher format.

Hard disc drives with a capacity of 500GB are now common.

The Hard Disc Revealed

You won't normally see your computer's hard disc, although you'll probably hear it, spinning away at several thousand revolutions per minute inside your computer's case.

An internal hard disc drive with the casing removed

Software on the Hard Disc

The hard disc is your computer's library where all of your software is saved, recorded permanently on the magnetic surfaces of the disc. When you launch, i.e. start a program, it is temporarily copied into the RAM or main memory of the computer, where it's available for use by the processor, as described earlier. The software on the hard disc includes the operating system such as Windows 7 and any programs you've installed, such as Microsoft Office or a photo editing program such as Adobe Photoshop Elements, for example. *Installing software* means copying a program from the manufacturer's CDs or DVDs then configuring it and saving it on your hard disc.

Modern software requires a lot of hard disc space; Microsoft specify that Windows 7 requires 16GB of free space on the hard disc. Adobe recommend at least 1.5GB of available hard disc space for the popular Photoshop Elements software.

Data on the Hard Disc

The hard disc is the place where all of the work you create is saved. For example, the text of a letter, report or book or all of your digital photographs and favourite music tracks and videos.

Each item of data that you save on the hard disc is known as a *file*; you give each file a name and a *file name extension* is added automatically. For example, a short story might be saved as **ghostlytale.docx**, with **.docx** indicating a document created in Microsoft Word 2010. A photograph might be saved as **party.jpg**, where **.jpg** is a common photographic file format.

Ideally the data files on your hard disc should be organised into a hierarchy of meaningful categories or *folders*, as shown on the right. This should make it easier to find and retrieve data at a later time. You can create more folders or *sub-folders* within a folder. For example, the **Holidays** folder on the right could be sub-divided into **Portugal**, **Scotland** and **Ireland** for example, to include your photographs from different holiday destinations.

Although sometimes referred to as *permanent memory*, the data on the hard disc can easily be deleted, either deliberately or accidentally. It's essential, therefore, to make *backup copies* of important documents or photographs, etc., on a separate medium such as a CD or DVD. The *flash drive* is a simple plug-in form of storage, ideal for making quick copies of files from the hard disc. For larger backups, *external hard disc drives* are available which simply plug into a port or socket on the computer. Hard disc drives of 150 — 500GB are typical on new computers and you can even get drives of 1TB (terabyte or 1000GB). A replacement or second hard disc drive can be bought for around £30 — £65, depending on the size.

A flash drive

PATA and SATA Hard Disc Drives

The internal hard disc revolves at high speed, taking its electrical power from one of the multi-coloured cables coming from the computer's power supply unit. Data from the hard disc is transferred to and from the memory via one of two types of cable.

The PATA or IDE Cable

This is an earlier design, a flat ribbon cable about one and a half inches wide, formerly known as IDE and now called PATA. The PATA cable allows two hard disc drives to be connected on one cable, in what is known as the *master/slave* configuration. The master is the primary drive used when the computer starts up and for subsequent running, while the secondary slave is used for additional storage.

The SATA Cable

This is a newer type of cable, bright red in colour, much less bulky than the PATA cable and designed to give better data transfer speed.

Each SATA drive has its own separate cable and modern motherboards have sockets to connect up to four SATA drives. It's possible to select which SATA drive is used to start or "boot up" the computer.

Formatting a New or Faulty Hard Disc Drive

A new hard disc has to be prepared for use by a process known as *formatting*; this process may also be used to repair a faulty hard disc. Formatting involves *wiping* the entire contents of the hard disc, so that any software and data files are removed. Hence the need to keep your original software CDs and DVDs and to make backup copies of all important data files, so that the contents of the hard disc can be restored to their original state.

Expansion Cards

The graphics components on your computer may be "on-board" i.e. built into the motherboard, the main printed circuit board of the computer shown on the next page; alternatively a separate graphics *expansion card*, as shown below, may be plugged into the motherboard.

An expansion card used to control the display of graphics

To display Windows 7 at its best, you need relatively powerful graphics facilities, compatible with a technical specification known as DirectX 9. The graphics card should also have at least 128MB of built-in memory of its own. The NVIDIA GeForce card shown above has 256MB of on-board memory and fits into a special graphics slot on the motherboard.

The latest type of graphics slot is known as PCI-Express and this superseded the earlier AGP slot. PCI-Express cards are quite different from standard PCI cards and are not interchangeable, so care should be taken when ordering new components. New motherboards are supplied with at least one PCI-Express slot for a graphics card and several empty PCI slots, shown as five whitish vertical rectangles on the next page; these standard PCI slots may be used to add facilities such as extra USB ports. It's quite feasible to fit an expansion card yourself — it just pushes into a motherboard slot and is retained by a single screw or clip.

The Motherboard

This is the main circuit board to which every other component of the computer is connected in some way. Some components plug directly into sockets on the motherboard while peripheral devices such as printers and monitors connect via cables.

The motherboard into which all other components are connected

In the motherboard above, the white rectangular area on the middle right is the socket for the processor. On the left-hand side of the socket there is a lever used to release the processor chip itself. The five vertical white rectangles on the left are the PCI slots for expansion cards, such as a sound card. The brown slot to the right of the five white slots is an AGP slot for a graphics card. The long, blue, rectangular strips near the bottom right of the motherboard are slots for the plug-in memory modules. The white clips which retain the memory modules are visible at each end of the two memory slots.

Data travels between the various components such as the memory and the processor along wires built into the motherboard. These wire "highways" are known as the *data bus*.

Jargon at a Glance

Byte The amount of memory required to store, for example, a letter of the alphabet or a keyboard character.

CPU Cache Special memory, within the processor, used to speed up the computer by keeping frequently used data in close proximity.

Data Bus The "highway" of fine wires along which data travels.

Dual-core processor Two processor cores on a single chip.

Expansion card A printed circuit board which plugs into a slot in the motherboard, e.g. to provide better graphics or sound facilities.

Formatting A process used to prepare a new hard disc drive or to repair a faulty drive, "wiping" any existing software or data files.

Gigabyte (GB) Approximately 1000 MB.

Gigahertz A measure of the speed of a processor.

Hard Disc Drive A set of high speed magnetic discs on a spindle, used to *permanently* store software and data files. SATA drives are the latest design, succeeding PATA drives, formerly known as IDE.

Kilobyte (K) 1024 bytes.

Megabyte (MB) Unit of measure for memory or hard disc storage capacity. 1 megabyte is approximately 1 million bytes.

Memory (RAM) A module or strip of microchips used to *temporarily* store the programs and data during the current computing session.

Motherboard The large printed circuit board, inside a computer, to which the other components are connected.

Operating system A suite of programs, such as Windows 7, in overall control of all aspects of the computer.

Processor (CPU) A chip, usually called the "brains" of the computer, used for all calculating, sorting and processing tasks.

Program A set of instructions or commands which enable the computer to perform tasks such as word processing or calculating.

Terabyte (TB) 1000GB.

Index